GOOD GARDENS BY DESIGN

GOOD GARDENS
BY DESIGN

The Principles of Classic Planning and Plant Selection

Donald Chilvers

Foreword by Sir John Mills CBE
Introduction by Peter Johnson
Additional photography by Lucy Dickens

Quiller Press

Copyright © 2005 Donald Chilvers

Photographs © Lucy Dickens and Donald Chilvers

First published in the UK in 2005
by Quiller Press, an imprint of Quiller Publishing Ltd

British Library Cataloguing-in-Publication Data
A catalogue record for this book is available from the British Library

ISBN 1 904057 71 3

Reproduction and typesetting by PDQ Digital Media Solutions Ltd., Bungay, Suffolk.
Text/jacket design by Caz Jones.

Printed in Italy

Quiller Press
An imprint of Quiller Publishing Ltd
Wykey House, Wykey, Shrewsbury, SY4 1JA
Tel: 01939 261616 Fax: 01939 261606
E-mail: info@quillerbooks.com
Website: www.swanhillbooks.com

CONTENTS

INTRODUCTION: THE CONNECTION BETWEEN ART AND GARDEN DESIGN by Peter Johnson

CHAPTER I
CASE STUDIES   8

CHAPTER II
LESSONS LEARNED:
ELEMENTS OF GARDEN MAKING   80

CHAPTER III
PLANTING SELECTION   106

CHAPTER IV
BORDER DESIGN   126

PREFACE

Gardens, gardens, and we are gardeners…
Razored hedgerow, flowers, those planted trees
Whose avenues conduct a greater ease
Of shadow to your own ladies' skins
And tilt this Nature to magnificence
And natural delight. But pardon us,
My Lord, if we reluctantly admit
Our horticulture not the whole of it,
Forgetting, that for you, this elegance
Is not our work, but your far tidier Sense.

Douglas Dunn, 'Gardeners', 1789

My interest in gardening goes back to childhood. Two people stand out in my memory. The first is Ada Burrow, a retired art teacher from Westmoreland who instilled in me and my brothers an unconscious love of gardening. She had a smallish garden, very little money, but a genius for imparting information. At the age of six I knew the names of all her apple trees (James Grieve, Reverend W. Wilks, Bramley's Seedling, Blenheim Orange, Codlin and Worcester Pearmain) and observed the way she achieved round, kaleidoscopic displays of annuals (using a large sieve upside down, through which she dropped the seed) and perennials. She was prepared to give us carte blanche at the top of her garden among the espalier pears. Here we sowed various garish annuals bought from Woolworths; the most pleasing was the linum mixed with nasturtium.

The other inspirational figure was Bert Wright, a retired colonial servant who was a stickler for discipline – spades had to be cleaned, tools put away in strict order, plans were drawn up for each season, regimented borders. I was his proud helper in the years up to about 12. His personality was suited to the role of employing and inspiring a young boy. He took infinite pains to achieve perfection. I remember he had planned to lay a wide brick path with a herringbone pattern the full length of his 100-yard garden.

Anyone who has done this will know that it involves making a vast number of triangular quarter bricks for the edges, which he did with a special bow saw. A lesson in perseverance! Most grown-ups run out of conversation while dealing with small boys but he never did; he had a way of treating me as an equal. Discussions about the course of the war or the faults of a relative or friend were never clouded with an assumption of superior knowledge on his part. As far as I can remember, he never showed or paid me thanks – that was not his way. We just had a firm, friendly relationship based on an implicit mutual regard and understanding.

This book describes my experiences of designing my own garden, together with the knowledge gained from the unexpected development of my second career – from an interested amateur to a landscape consultant. The idea for this book was proposed by a client who suggested that I should document the gardens I had constructed to see what lessons could be learned. My approach to designing is based on the traditional values preached by Mrs Jekyll of integration of the house with the gardens. An air of tranquillity and simplicity is sought in my garden designs – like Mrs Jekyll, I deplore 'silly fashions' which serve only to destroy an otherwise harmonious garden.

The text is confined mainly to ornamental gardens, excluding vegetables, orchards and woodlands. However, brief mention is made of these horticultural groups while describing case studies of planting schemes and the selection and grouping of plants examined in the last chapter. Predominantly my experience has been restricted to gardens of calcareous soil consistencies rather than acidic conditions – rhododendrons and azaleas sadly are not my staple diet (a bias reflected by the selection of plants at the end of this book). I make no apology for giving so much space to my own garden – it was the blueprint used for other garden designs. The plans drawn up for each client are influenced by the design originals of my garden, in a number of cases simplified to enhance clarity of form and order. My aim is to show what can be accomplished through the building of a garden.

Donald Chilvers
January 2005

FOREWORD

Why do we treasure our garden? Mary and I have always loved ours for its sense of space and the opportunity it offers for retreating into a world which is different: 'The busy world is hushed.'

Hundreds of new gardening books appear on the shelves every year but this one, called *Good Gardens by Design* by my great friend Donald Chilvers, is out on its own.

It is obviously impossible for one book to deal with all aspects of gardening, but what I like about Donald's approach is that he limits himself to those plans, plants and features which emerge from his own work files. His results should inspire his readers as they show what can be done with quite unpromising sites. He has designed many beautiful gardens and very generously donated all the money to charity.

I felt our garden at Hills House was superb, but he came up with three miraculous adjustments which added greatly to our enjoyment.

Happy reading. Happy looking.

Sir John Mills CBE

Sir John Mills — Climber

ACKNOWLEDGEMENTS

I wish to acknowledge the forbearance of my clients who encouraged me to take photographs and describe the progress and evolution of their gardens: Mr & Mrs Christopher Clarke; Mrs David Clive; Mr & Mrs Michael Coghlan; Mrs Tony Davies; Mr & Mrs Barnaby Dickens; Ms Marlene Edwards; The Hon. Sir Timothy & Lady Elworthy; Mrs Reg East; Mr & Mrs Peter Fox; Mr & Mrs Toby Gawith; Mr & Mrs Andrew Holmes; Mr & Mrs Peter Horbye; Mr & Mrs Rudi Krefting; Mr & Mrs Alan Lamb; Sir John & Lady Mills; Mr & Mrs Jonathan Pelly-Fry; General & Mrs Michael Tennant; Mr & Mrs Ian Wylie; Mr & Mrs Peter Worth.

Thanks also to Mrs Thomas Kressner (who permitted us to photograph her pool and surroundings) and the Dowager Countess Cawdor (Cawdor Castle).

The photography, with very few exceptions, is of the gardens on which I have worked. Most of the shots were taken by the talented photographer, Lucy Dickens. Her mastery of the art of plant close-ups is unique.

Many writers have given me inspiration especially John Brooks, Diane Saville, G.C. Taylor, Rosemary Verey, Gertrude Jekyll and lastly, my one-time neighbour and friend, the late David Hicks.

Thanks are due to Peter Johnson and Jessica Laflin who edited the book.

I also received assistance from Lyn Corson, Gillian Bauer (landscape designer), and from friends who reviewed the early drafts: Bill Birch Reynardson, Joanna Peppiat, Gillian Newbery, Mary Sandys, John Chater and Cassie Bassett.

I would also like to acknowledge the help provided by the following: Blackwood Nurseries, Southridge, Berks; Woodbridge Nurseries, Longworth, Oxon; Nottcutts, Nuneham Courtenay, Oxon; Beales Roses, Attleborough, Norfolk; Maurice Mandry, Ottershaw, Surrey (trees and hedging); Holley Hextall, Calne, Wiltshire (stone supplier).

The most significant help of all has been provided by my wife, Rosie, whose opinion and support has been vital to the success of all the projects undertaken.

William Nicholson (1872–1949), *Gertrude Jekyll's Boots* (reproduced by permission of Elizabeth Banks © Tate).

INTRODUCTION
The Connection between
Art and Garden Design

Peter Johnson

Steps at Frant Court,
Sussex

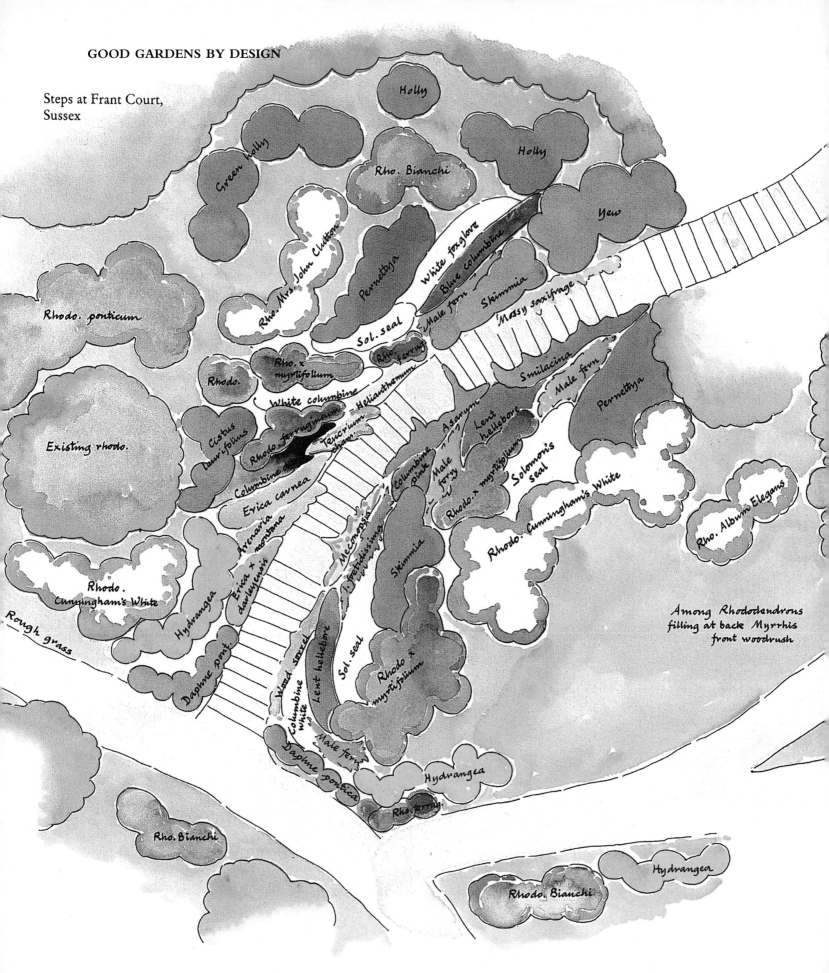

Holly

Green holly

Rho. Bianchi

Holly

Yew

Rhodo. ponticum

Rho. Mrs John Clutton

Pernettya

White foxglove

Blue columbine

Male fern

Skimmia

Mossy saxifrage

Sol. seal

Rho. ferrug

Rho. x myrtifolium

Smilacina

Male fern

Pernettya

Rhodo.

White columbine

Teucrium

Helianthemum

Asarum

Lent hellebore

Solomon's seal

Cistus
laurifolius

Male
ferry

Rhodo ferruginum

Columbine d

Erica carnea

Arenaria

Meconopsis

Columbine
pink

Skimmia

Rhodo. x myrtifolium

Rhodo. Cunningham's White

Rho. Album Elegans

Existing rhodo.

Erica × darleyensis

montana

I. speciodissima

Rhodo.
Cunningham's White

Hydrangea

Daphne pont.

Wood sorrel

Lent hellebore

Sol. seal

Rhodo x myrtifolium

Among Rhododendrons
filling at back Myrrhis
front woodrush

Rough grass

Columbine
white

Male fern

Daphne pontica

Rho. ferrug

Hydrangea

Rho. Bianchi

Hydrangea

Rhodo. Bianchi

Mrs Jekyll's planting plan for a flight of steps demonstrates her unique blending of colours and shapes. (Illustration by Liz Pepperell, copyright © Frances Lincoln Ltd 1992, taken from *The Gardens of Gertrude Jekyll* by Richard Bisgrove. Reproduced by permission of Frances Lincoln Limited, 4 Torriano Mews, Torriano Avenue, London NW5 2RZ.)

Claude's (17th-century) landscapes, based on his imagination *not* reality, created a 'man-made' countryside – grass, clumps of trees, streams, low hills, irregular lakes. Brown added focal points and ha-has to such compositions, achieving both beauty and balance. (Claude, *Landscape with the Marriage of Isaac and Rebekah* ('*The Mill*'), oil on canvas. © The National Gallery, London.)

It is interesting to realise that good gardens by design have been a feature in this country for more than 200 years. Donald Chilvers believes that by concentrating on the effect of making a garden a beautiful haven – as it should be – we will experience both aesthetic and occupational pleasure, as decreed since the dawn of civilisation.

Donald has been particularly inspired by Persian artistic rug and carpet patterns influenced by garden design (see page 84). These artistic forms may serve to illustrate the importance mankind has placed upon the garden, determining its inspirational qualities found in symmetrical and structured design or natural-looking grounds, far removed from the hectic and expanding world. Thus, the garden is perceived as a medium for art, a living canvas similar to an oil painting, an entity in itself where one seeks solitude and beauty, and where ideas are fashioned to influence other creative methods, like design, painting and sculpture.

Before photography and travel made it possible for us to view some of the great gardens in distant lands and towns, paintings were a main source of inspiration for garden workers. A few paintings included in this book portray the importance of the medium and serve to remind us of the successive development of garden architecture in Britain over the last 250 years.

The connection between art and gardening is historic. Even Capability Brown, the dictator of British garden style, had in his mind's eye a Claude Lorraine painting when designing his renowned Arcadian landscapes. However, the history of the ha-ha and vistas precedes the magic of Capability Brown and can be seen in the work of Thomas Robins. Lord Dickenson's garden at Painswick House, Gloucestershire, is one such example, where two of Robins' enchanting vistas are encountered ending with irregular follies that allow the two façades to be enjoyed.

Repton's design for Sheringham Hall (taken from the *Red Book*). Note the follies, statues, tree plantings and terrace (photo courtesy Arthur Ackermann & Peter Johnson Limited).

Brown died in 1783 and for decades his works dictated the form for major gardens, sweeping away the earlier stiff formality, developing 'naturalism' on the grand scale in its place. He greatly influenced Humphry Repton, even though the classically romanticised and spacious landscape concept of Brown remained. Repton progressed closer to the house, introducing formality through geometric flower borders, steps, shrubberies, terraces, flower and cottage ornamental gardens, and balustrades, which are still popular today. His watercolours became a key element in selling his design services to prominent figures competing to convey their influence, prestige and wealth to others; these he bound together within his *Red Books*, accompanied by garden plans and ideas. He prepared detailed paintings of each garden, creating an image of what the client would view after the design process had been concluded. These two painted stages allowed his clients (beginning in Norfolk but then spreading much further afield) to grasp how their gardens and estates would develop visually in the same way that Donald Chilvers produces modern designs for his clients. Happily these *Red Books* still exist today and may be used to inspire other likeminded garden designers.

The prominent figure, William Robinson, closely followed Repton. He was a peasant boy from Ireland who became a highly influential figure in garden design, founding the influential and hugely successful *The Garden* magazine in 1871. He also wrote various books and articles advising others on the general principles of garden design, such as *The Wild Garden* (1870) and *The English Flower Garden* (1883), informing readers of current design fashions. His love for cottage gardens and informal styles of smaller estates imbued his followers, including Gertrude Jekyll and Vita Sackville-West, with a zeal for new ways of garden making. Once Robinson had established himself he purchased a large estate, Gravetye Manor in Sussex, and devoted much time to creating a garden there. He died aged 95 in 1935, publishing his outspoken ideas to the end.

As with Humphry Repton's *Red Books*, Robinson's works gave design, arrangement and technical garden advice. However, they differed through their portrayal of the aesthetic taste and sentiment applied to the avant-garde and Arts and Crafts movement, where awareness and feeling for nature was predominant.

In 1930, Vita Sackville West and her husband Harold Nicolson, bought Sissinghurst Castle (Kent) and turned a neglected wilderness into a garden, following a style of 'the strictest formality and design' with the 'maximum informality in planting'. Its success is one of the legends of garden making and is regarded as the most important current influence, perhaps only matched by Hidcote Manor near Chipping Campden, Gloucestershire, which was laid out by the American, Major Johnston, just before the First World War. Major Johnston was the first to opt for mixed borders, including shrubs, which are common plants today. He, like Donald Chilvers, segregated the garden into 'outdoor rooms', which later appeared so effectively in the designs of Vita Sackville-West and Mrs Jekyll.

Gertrude Jekyll was born into an artistic family. Her talents as a craftswoman and painter informed her early career. It was not until she was in her 50s, when her eyesight was failing, that she turned from painting to designing gardens. As happened to Vita Sackville-West, the naturalistic and wild character of Robinson's garden designs affected this talented lady. She was similarly interested in avant-garde art,

Cottage at Ellen's Green, Near Cranley, Surrey by James Matthews (photo courtesy Arthur Ackermann & Peter Johnson Limited).

The picture of Loseley Court (Surrey) by Thomas Hunt is a good example of the 'jolly hollyhocks' style of painting giving dramatic emphasis to entrances and exits – a point taken up by Donald Chilvers time and again in the case studies in this book (photo courtesy Arthur Ackermann & Peter Johnson Limited).

knowing both John Ruskin and William Morris. The influence these particular figures had upon her artistic style is very obvious through her detailed embroidery, wood and metal works. Additionally, Turner's work she much admired through his raw impression of the wildness and beauty of nature, where colour and movement worked to rally the senses – a sentiment she applied to her impressionistic flowerbeds during her design career.

Not only did she develop a totally new way of gardening, but she also prompted people to think about their garden with views from their house windows. Likewise, Donald Chilvers seeks a unified and harmonising whole picture. It was during this period that many artists started painting flowerbeds galore (which could be described as 'jolly hollyhocks'). Gertrude Jekyll was different – she used her artist's eye to produce the colour and composition we have all grown to admire. Single-coloured borders of grey- and silver-leafed plants were used with the blending colours and backgrounds, much as a painter would do; these were her fortes. Her partnership with Lutyens spanned many years during which time they designed approximately 30 gardens.

It must be remembered that the Jekyll/ Robinson/ Sackville-West brigade did not exist in isolation. They were all part of the Arts and Crafts movement, where art and literature amalgamated to inspire and enthuse, drawing upon mythology, legend and nature, when people desired the resurrection of dying traditions and folk crafts. This artistic circle was also influenced by the overseas traditions of the Japanese, Italian, French, American and Persian, developing and incorporating many of the designs and ideas into British design, which can still be seen today.

I shall give a brief summary of the important attributes of these foreign traditions which have served to influence not only our predecessors, but the designers of today. One naturally associates a Japanese garden with almond blossom, flower-laden plums, cherry trees with wisteria, paeonia, maples and much colour. The Japanese have always given preference to proportion rather than colour; they need to cope with smaller spaces than most, so it is almost like planning a composition in a confined space, giving a sense of colour and separateness from the busy world outside. In Italy, terraces, walls, big earthenware pots, loggias, statuary and tall cypress trees are the ingredients for a pleasing garden design. There are fewer flowers, perhaps because it has a hotter and drier climate. France has produced avenues of elegant trees, carpet bedding, great terraces and fountains, which play their part in formalising the garden and the house. Wrought iron balustrades and balconies also come into the frame. America has a little of everything, borrowing influences from all the European garden traditions and also, especially on the West Coast, taking much from Japan. Palms, oleanders and other such tropical plants can be found in the warmer climes, but in the Northern States, the gardens might have come straight from the pen of Jekyll or Robinson; at their best they are a match for any in the world.

This rapid review of the history of garden making may assist readers in their understanding of what has influenced designers. I am hoping it will also encourage them to create gardens of their own, befitting their tastes and desires, while drawing upon these great figures in garden design for inspiration. Even though the great craftsmen of the past age worked on large estates, and in their heyday worked with big budgets, there is no need for anyone to feel overawed and downcast – there could not be a greater contrast with the modest contexts in which Donald Chilvers has worked. The scale may change but the principles still hold good.

Peter Johnson
Arthur Ackermann & Peter Johnson Limited
Fine Art Dealers (London)

I

CHAPTER I

Case Studies

THE OLD RECTORY
The geometrically designed garden

One of the most delightful things about a garden is the anticipation it provides.

W.F. Watts

'Before'

The Old Rectory is a beautiful Georgian house surrounded by fine countryside scattered with distant trees. First encounters suggested the property cried out for a rear garden of geometric design. Gravel paths, clipped hedges, walls and symmetrical flower beds were needed to create a balanced structure. However, the success of this scheme depended on the maintenance of that geometry through regular hedge clipping, perennial border maintenance and grass cutting. We wished to recreate the past glory and ambience of the grounds by recalling the English rectory garden – an image which conjures up striped lawns, croquet hoops, herbaceous borders and spreading walnut or cedar trees, and those far-off days when the rectory garden, shared by parishioners, had a gardener to enhance the priest's horticultural efforts.

When we took over the Old Rectory at Brightwell Baldwin, any past glories in the garden were no longer evident. The house sat in a virtually empty green space to the south and was flanked by rather large trees to the east and west (see the photograph bottom left). To the north could be glimpsed a park, the design of which is attributed to Repton. The front of the house was classical but rather stark but the situation of the property provided an exceptional view over distant fields, so our initial design work focused on its preservation.

Major redesigning was needed and we were determined to achieve a sufficiently high standard for the garden to be included in the National Gardens Scheme's *Gardens of England and Wales Open for Charity* (affectionately known as *The Yellow Book*) within six years – an ambitious project! The architectural character of the house would have to shape any architectural treatment of the garden. Formality was essential in the areas adjacent to the Georgian house.

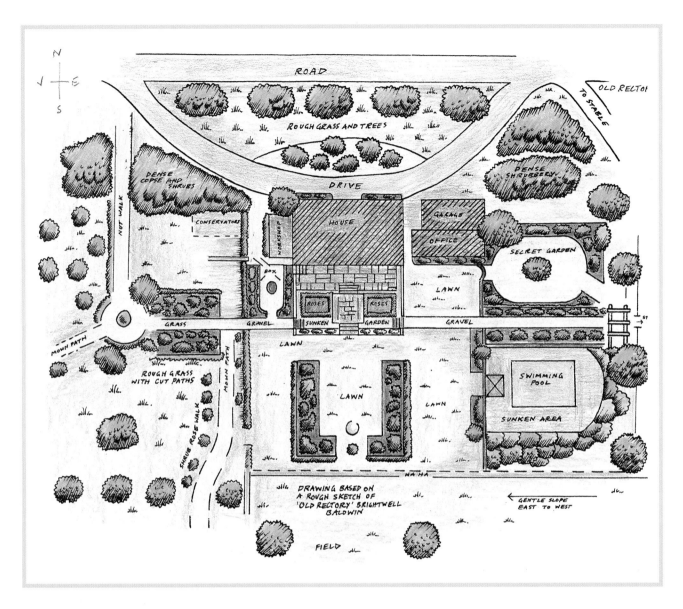

Axial lines based on the principal doors, walls and windows were used as the foundation for dividing the garden. Our intention to excavate a swimming pool was also taken into account. Also, there was scope for excavation close to the rear of the house so that the terrain and views from the south-looking basement rooms could be improved. The design plan illustrates how we created 'rooms' in the garden, each with distinct characteristics and plant associations. This was achieved by erecting a series of walls and hedges (which took their alignment from the house itself) to provide protection to quite an exposed area. A ha-ha or sunken fence was used to deter invasion from farm animals without the need for fencing on the south perimeter.

Secret garden to the east (Room 1)

Room 1 is a secret garden created towards the east to block views of the stables. We planted a large **Portugal laurel** and surrounded it with a circular bed of white **shasta daisies** and a lawn of similar shape. This area was bordered by the taller **hebes**, *Buddleja alternifolia,* **spireas**, *Viburnum tinus* and **ceanothus Italian Skies**, in front of which were **hostas, alchemillas, geraniums, sisyrinchiums** and evergreen **epimediums**.

Swimming pool (Room 2)

Room 2 was chosen for the swimming pool area and had to be levelled before excavation commenced. The image of the banked flowerbed beyond the swimming pool shows where we filled it with herbs, consisting of **sage** (grey, yellow and blue varieties), **thyme** and other herb varieties. Recently two artichokes have been added for vertical emphasis. Pink roses **(The Fairy)** were also planted at the back, along with the **Rothschild cotoneaster** to the far right. The rear hedge was made from a sizeable evergreen and large-leaved **escallonia (macrantha)**, which is neat for most of the year and yields a beautiful pink flower towards the end of the summer.

Descending terraces at the rear of the house (Room 3)

Adjoining the back of the house is Room 3 which became a series of descending terraces created by excavating earth, thereby improving the view from the lower ground kitchen. Large quantities of York stone kerbstones were used to create a succession of different levels. The lower terraces were composed of **lavender**, creeping **hebes** *(Hebe pinguifolia)*, **caryopteris, aubretia** and some **roses** surrounded by **box**. These various honey-like scented plants are a great addition because they attract bees, thereby aiding pollination in the garden. We placed two cast iron Victorian vases at the base of the steps and two *Juniperus communis* at the top of the centre steps to create a dramatic exit from the rear of the house up to the top lawn.

A photograph taken from the bottom of the sunken garden alongside the kitchen shows what an inspiring picture results from the grey colour-coordinated planting and stones topped with grey slates of the pavilion. By digging out the sunken garden, we were effectively eroding the foundations of the listed house so the side was buttressed. Drainage was also an important consideration. Additionally, to the west side of the house, we planted a parterre of pink **rose** beds lined by **box** hedging and backed this up with **ceanothus** and **cistus** below – an aromatic exit to the front drive!

Classic borders (Room 4)

This is a classic herbaceous bordered lawn area with a quick-growing combination of *Lonicera nitida* and **Myrobalan plum** (which gives the effect of box hedging) planted behind the borders. On the east of Room 4, a wall and summerhouse were constructed from old bricks, the latter doubling as a changing room on the pool side. (See page 15 for the planting scheme.)

The informal area – rose walk and orchard (Room 5)

To the west of the house lies a line of substantial **hornbeam** trees with an orchard beyond, whose presence dominated both practical and aesthetic considerations. The removal of several of these trees allowed a natural frame to be arranged which draws the eye to important picturesque views such as the village church. Winding paths were cut through the rough grass, bordered by the odd shrub such as *Exochorda macrantha*, *Viburnum opulus* and **shrub roses** in big groups.

In the orchard we built a hexagonal wooden gazebo to provide an interesting focal point within a dull area – it also gives the grandchildren a place to hide and play. Surprisingly, it was simple to construct, cost little, and will last forever, having been built with treated timber. Alongside the structure **pampas grasses** were planted to accentuate the area's rustic atmosphere. On the left, climbing an apple tree, a mixture of white roses **(Rambling Rector)** and pink roses **(American Pillar)** was added (which have scaled about 30ft/9.1m in four years). Between the gazebo and the field a row of **Italian alders** was planted to frame the scene and provide protection from the prevailing southwest wind.

Axial paths

A photograph taken from the east side of the sunken garden shows that the gravelled central path is the axis point. Its gradual downhill decline is flanked with clipped, various hued, prostrate **junipers**. These plants are often disparaged, yet they, together with the little **box** hedges around the **Silver Jubilee roses,** provide great interest and colour in the winter months. Similarly, the circular bed of **santolina**, seen to the right side of the image, is equally attractive. Additionally, beyond the hedge in the distance, may be seen the beautiful shape of *Robinia pseudoacacia* and the outline cast by **hornbeam** trees and the winter-flowering **cherry** (closer to the hedge). It is interesting to note that these huge hornbeams were the result of leaving an old hornbeam hedge to re-grow; how quickly they grew after a few wet winters, with their flowers a joy to behold in late summer!

A photograph taken from the west of the same axial path conveys how the eastern end was developed aesthetically by placing putti on either side. This image was intensified by planting rows of *Juniperus communis* interspaced with **lavender, catmint** and **potentilla (Elizabeth)** beyond. At the far end is a pergola which provides a turning point when moving towards the swimming pool, secret garden and stable areas.

The vertical elements of the original garden were sparse; just three or four thorns and a cherry tree to the right (which was removed because it interfered with the larger plan). This landscape defect was overcome in stages. First, pergolas were built at the extreme ends of the central path, followed by a planting of **crab apples**, **weeping pears** and tall shrubs. Two **Irish yews** were planted in the centre of the ha-ha, together with two semi-mature **chestnuts** which were positioned further away in the field.

The front

In the front garden, quite an austere style was adopted. A very large evergreen *Magnolia grandiflora* was placed against the corner of the house, which echoed the building's height and softened its western profile. Against the house a **yew** hedge was planted to form a buttress that over time would grow to the height of our tall front windows. To emphasise the start of the steps, a low **hebe (subalpina)** fronted by a row of **santolina (Edward Bowles)** and two **box** balls were aligned against the structure. Opposite the front door we planted a bank of *Viburnum bodnantense* fronted by a deep bed of **polygonum** of the largest variety **(knotweed)**. This picturesque image was completed with drums of **yew** that framed both sides of the driveway.

Planting schemes

A planting scheme needed to be developed to provide interest throughout the year in each room. A succession of feature plants against a relatively unchanging pattern of hedges was arranged. Shrubs and bulbs **(aconites, daffodils** and **snowdrops)** were massed in the orchard and front areas. In the herbaceous borders perennials were used, which collectively yield blooms over relatively long periods – from spring-flowering **hesperis** to the **Michaelmas daisies** that see the garden through the first frost.

For example in the twin borders:

Winter	The effervescent polished green of **choisya** and the red-berried fronds of the *Cotoneaster latifolia*.
Early spring	Pink **poppies**, white **hesperis** and the leafing **cornus**.
Early summer	**Geraniums**, pink **roses** en masse, **sages, campanula, achillea (The Pearl)** and **gypsophila**.
Midsummer	**Phlox, lavandulas, herbaceous clematis, penstemon** and **echinops**.
Late summer	Big patches of creamy **sedum Autumn Joy** (beautiful when they catch dew drops), **Michaelmas daisies, acanthus, agapanthus** and the climax of **rue**.
Late autumn	The best time of the horticultural year with a full spectrum of grey to green. A variety of grey-green **phlomis**, olive **sage**, silver, pink and yellow toned, bluish-green **rue** backed with the roseate foliage of *Kolkwitzia amabilis* **(Beauty Bush)**, the peachy presence of **cornus**, and finally the plum-coloured patches of **sedum Autumn Joy** complete an autumnal composition.

Conclusions

Gardening at the Rectory and working inside a strong framework was an easier task compared to that of a wilder location, like the naturalistic cottage garden. The property is quite exposed and its soil has a high alkaline content so plants have difficulty surviving. This problem was addressed through the provision of high hedges and the introduction of plants that can withstand the climate.

Fifteen years later it is interesting to look back upon our work at the Rectory. We needed to alter the apparent shape of the garden by accentuating its length outwards from the back of the house. Vertical elements also had to be introduced. Some mistakes were made. I wish the paths had been wider and the ha-ha deepened – at 3½ feet (106cm), it is high enough to contain sheep but not to deter a herd of determined cows!

EWELME
A cottage at the top of a slope

A garden makes all our senses swim with pleasure.

William Lawson

'Before'

I was invited to the historic village of Ewelme to visit an unadorned cottage situated on a steep incline. My senses 'swam with pleasure' at the exciting possibilities this sloping site would present, particularly as the property faced southwest. Near the house there was an opportunity to extend the indoor space by laying a flat terrace and by a series of retaining walls to level and style individually the spaces below. Additionally, a steep path could be laid for use by barrows and mowers that would allow access to hidden areas beyond the terrace. There was an evident prospect for dramatic planting.

I was asked to design a garden at this newly refurbished cottage with the intention of making it 'instantly mature' and 'of the sort that required little maintenance'. A vegetable patch was also desired. At the rear of the cottage is a rising field grazed by sheep. The dominance of this field was an imperative factor in the design; from its high, distant position, the garden could spring from the landscape like a lush, fertile oasis in the desert; plants had to be prudently selected to complement the garden's rural surroundings.

The garden was rectangular in shape with its eastern view spoiled by the roof of a cricket pavilion which jutted above the fence line. On its western side stood a wooden fence which the clients agreed should be replaced by a wall. The photograph conveys the unpromising view to the left, created by a plain, rear extension on the cottage. The garden's initial development stages can also be seen.

A plan was prepared involving the construction of two stone terraces at the rear of the cottage with a terraced lawn and steps adjoining the main stone terrace. From the lawn at the bottom of the site, the centre of the house can be approached through the centre of the garden up a flight of York stone steps edged with kerbstones and **santolina**. A long sloping path was added to the left of the garden with minimum

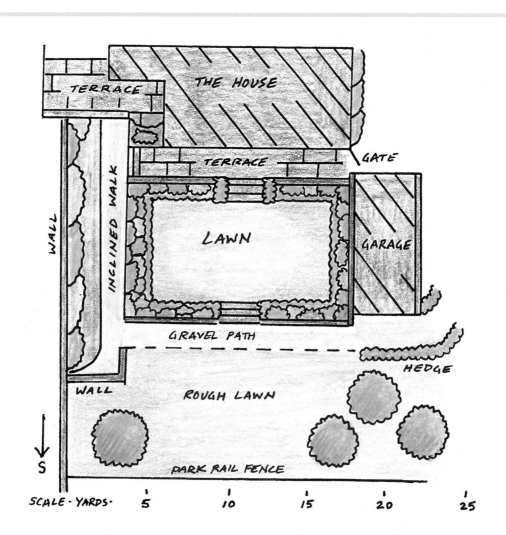

IN THIS EXAMPLE THE PLAN AND PERSPECTIVE SHOW A SCHEME PREPARED FOR A COTTAGE WITH A SLOPING SITE. IT AFFORDED AN OPPORTUNITY TO BUILD TWO STONE TERRACES. THERE WAS NO CALL FOR ANY FOCAL POINT AT THE BOTTOM OF THE GARDEN SINCE IT WAS A RURAL SCENE BEYOND. THE EARTH AT THE LOWER END OF THE PLOT WAS REMOVED TO THE TOP TERRACES SO AS TO CREATE LEVEL SURFACES IN EACH SUBDIVISION. THE NARROW BEDS IN THE LAWN TERRACE ARE USED FOR MAINLY GREY PLANTS WITH SOME LOW ROSES. THE BED AGAINST THE LEFT WALL IS FILLED WITH LARGE SHRUBS AND CLIMBERS EDGED WITH EUPHORBIAS ETC.

intermediate stone steps ascending to the drawing room in the left corner. A recessed terrace was also created in that top left corner of the plot. This sloping path facilitated the movement of machinery while providing an extra dimension for planting purposes.

To accentuate the subdivisions, earth at the lower end of the plot was levelled and removed to the top terraces. Great care was taken to preserve the topsoil during this process. At the southern perimeter, the old hedge was grubbed out and replaced with a line of park fencing so the gentle, rising field beyond would appear as an extension of the garden.

The narrow beds on the top terraces were filled mainly with grey plants and a number of low **roses**; the beds against the west wall were edged with **euphorbia** and **cistus**, backed with large shrubs such as **ceanothus** and the climbing *Clematis armandii*.

It was decided to use **Virginia creeper** to cover the back and side of the new house extension to disguise the transition from old to new building material. To the right side of this area, a mixed **lonicera** and *Prunus myrobalan* hedge was planted around the vegetable garden and a winter-flowering **cherry** was placed in front of the cricket pavilion roof.

To the extreme left corner, the 'secret garden' was fronted by *Euphorbia griffithii* and various climbing plants on the fence. Their position obstructed views of the property from the road and blocked the grim sight of an oil tank.

Conclusions

I had never tackled a hillside garden prior to Ewelme. I found the incorporation of steps and terraced walls most advantageous. But as Mrs Jekyll said: 'It is a good rule to make the steps so easy that one can run up and down them.' She would have been displeased by the steep gradient of our first group of steps! This was later rectified through the addition of an extra tread.

While working at the cottage, I was blessed with kind weather, a smooth progression of work and extremely relaxed clients. The photograph taken (in June) from halfway down the garden demonstrates the exuberant planting schemes.

19

MORETON FIELD

Creating a farmhouse garden from scratch

Our bodies are our gardens, to which our wills are gardeners.

William Shakespeare

In the village of Moreton, near Thame, a renovated brick farmhouse sat exposed upon a gently rising slope to the south. It stood apart from its surroundings; to rectify this problem, landscaping around its circumference and the creation of sheltered areas was needed. Our plan was eventually to establish a traditional farmhouse garden which could be seen from all rooms of the house.

I first saw the farmhouse in 1995. It had been recently bought and I was warned not to expect much: 'We have done the inside but the outside is a wilderness.' I was accompanied by Martin Bennett, a landscaping contractor and past business associate. The property was down a long, half-tarmaced farm track that ran through flat, waterlogged fields, while in the distance a line of 30-foot (9.1m) high Leylandii shadowed a small huddle of farm buildings. The farmhouse stood next to a large thatched barn and a path wound through the Leylandii to an ungainly porch which guarded the side door. 'This is just your cup of tea', Martin remarked, 'You can start with a clean slate!' This observation was not entirely true – an enormous willow situated to the corner of the dwelling, a brook beside a fence, and a fetching barn could all be incorporated into the design. The air was so cold that first day it could be gulped down like iced water; we nicknamed the house 'Wuthering Heights', more for the ambience than location.

The clients shared my dislike of the Leylandii and suggested its immediate removal (unfortunately we underestimated the plant's important defence against the northeast wind which occasionally buffets the house!). I produced a five-page report that recorded my initial impressions of the house and its surroundings, and suggested ways to improve the elevation of the building which included: (a) adding an architrave to the front door to stress its importance and (b) rebuilding the side entrance porch in a 'lighter' style. I also suggested that growing

Moreton Field

Notes

1) Shallow slope from south, excavate to achieve level terrace and lawn at back of house, using retaining walls and steps at circumference.

2) Make use of stream at south end with little bridge and victorian arches to create a focal point.

3) High shrubs at far end, to match victorian arches.

4) Create walks as shown.

5) Use walls at both ends of new terrace by house, to achieve privacy and protection from west winds.

6) Create rose garden later, in west division.

7) Improve door treatment on east and south sides. Victorian arches by drive.

8) Planting of yew and other evergreen hedges to emphasise divisions.

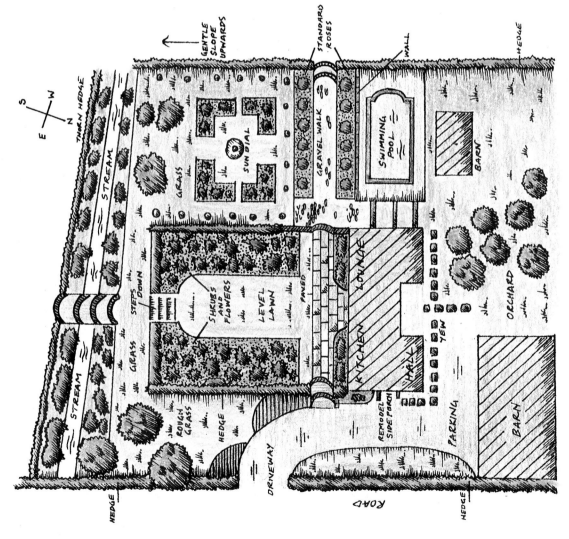

Virginia creeper against the house would make the walls look less forbidding at the back.

The schematic plan shows the main elements of the scheme.

The approach from the drive towards the front door needed to be made separate from the rest. Victorian iron arches were installed which, together with an added wall at both corners of the house front, provided privacy and shelter to those sitting in the main garden. I also suggested the construction of a York stone terrace at the side of the building with formal herbaceous gardens beyond. Some excavation on the (rising) sloping main garden to the south was desirable, so that two levels could be achieved with central steps leading to the higher level. Fortunately, a small stream beyond the new heightened level allowed for the creation of a bridge. Beyond this, an arch was installed and smothered with pink **roses**, making an attractive entrance from the field area.

Paths round the garden (and to the tennis court area) were designed to avoid the necessity to retrace steps. They are wide enough for two people to walk alongside each other.

Strict geometry prevailed in the design of the southern side garden where a rectangular compartment, some 25 feet (7.6m) across and 60 feet (18.2m) long, was levelled out and bordered by twin borders, each 15 feet (4.5m) wide. Repeated drifts of **stachys**, various herbaceous plants with a liking for damp conditions, and high shrubs at the back of the borders also created a sense of abundance and growth; their borders incorporated foliage of the softest colours – pink, white, lavender, purple and grey. Centrally placed stone steps provide a focal point in the middle of the southern garden, while the installation of a Victorian arched iron pergola at the far end of the back garden adds height beyond. Borders were created against the south and east sides of the house to soften its lines.

Old bricks with rounded capping stones were used for making walls, including those by the swimming pool (note the deep grouting gaps!), with the clusters of bright pink flowers of the **American Pillar rose** languishing in the corner.

Conclusions

The garden is achieving maturity since its construction nine years ago. The evergreen hedges behind the main borders have reached a height of 5 feet (152cm), while the big shrubs and trees to the south reflect the height of the Victorian metal arch. Time and structure have been the key ingredients for this successful garden.

The owners have introduced many personal additions including a superb barn conversion to the west of the house. This modification has greatly improved the perspective of the property in that direction. Furthermore, a garden design course stimulated the client's knowledge and enthusiasm for horticulture and evidently helped nurture the garden since my visit nine years ago.

PARSON'S REST

A Brecon bungalow

The size of the garden has nothing to do with it; twenty acres or one acre or half an acre, it is all the same.

Vita Sackville-West

'Before'

The art of garden design can be challenging when confronted with an undistinguished house. The Brecon property's front and rear gardens covered a diminutive, rectangular-shaped amount of ground, and its main orientation came from the east. Furthermore, a Leylandii hedge prevented light from entering the grounds.

The owners had moved from a glorious Dorset cottage and garden to a Brecon bungalow to be near their children. They were keen gardeners who had previously opened their cottage grounds to the public once a year. I was sent a plan and photographs and asked for my professional assistance.

I was astounded to learn that Gertrude Jekyll actually saw less than half of the 300 gardens she designed. She drafted plans from a property's dimensions and descriptions of setting, and corresponded with the landscaper by letter until work was complete. Consequently, many American clients never met their renowned garden designer. I now have shared this experience in some minuscule way!

My client's photos illustrated the orientation of the garden (awkwardly situated, facing east at the back of the house), the position of the doors and windows, and information about boundaries. In a telephone conversation we concluded that a terrace and summerhouse should be constructed against the south boundary (conveniently, a neighbour's garage wall) so the garden could radiate from this point. The design incorporated a planting scheme for each subsection of the small property. A trailer-load of the key shrubs and plants was purchased from a wholesale supplier and driven by the client's daughter to Wales.

The initial outline plan displays the main features of the design scheme. The photograph on page 26 shows the garden's initial development. From the garden's northern perspective, it is possible to see the south-facing summerhouse with a trellis and bower against the

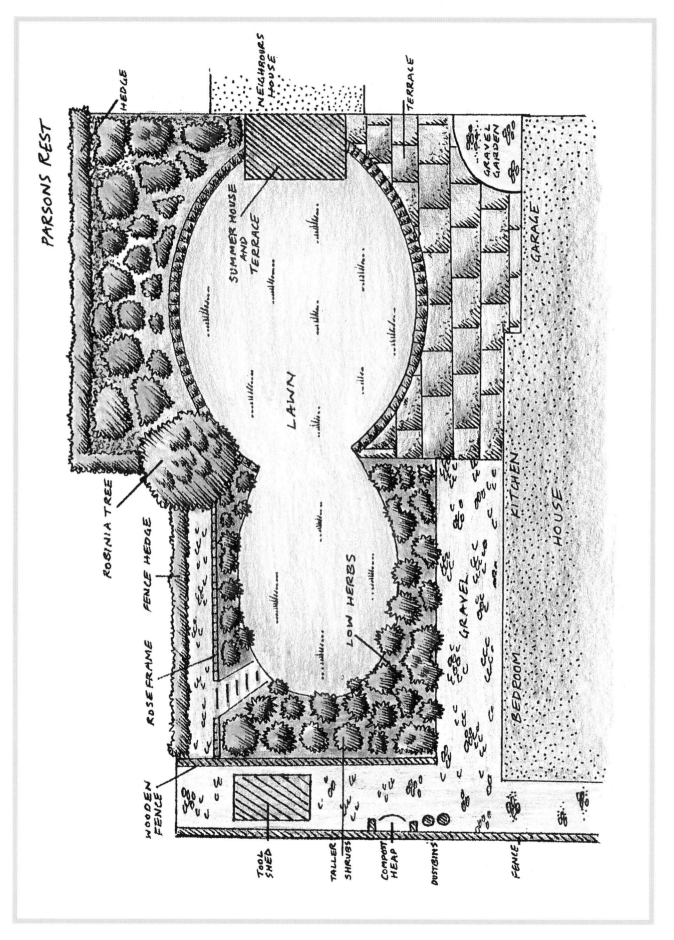

PARSONS REST

HEDGE

NEIGHBOURS HOUSE

TERRACE

GRAVEL GARDEN

SUMMER HOUSE AND TERRACE

LAWN

ROBINIA TREE

FENCE HEDGE

ROSE FRAME

WOODEN FENCE

LOW HERBS

GRAVEL

GARAGE

KITCHEN

BEDROOM

HOUSE

TOOL SHED

TALLER SHRUBS

COMPOST HEAP

DUSTBINS

FENCE

hedge; a gravel garden in the corner by the summerhouse was laid in addition to create variety. The rear hedge was to be cut back by approximately 5 feet (150cm) and reduced in height by the same amount. A side trellis fence was built as well as a bower which, within four years, was completely obscured by shrubs.

The clients wanted plant profusion of the loveliest sort and were prepared to remove, later, items that might grow too big as they matured. No opportunity for planting has been lost.

The colour theme for the bed in front of the trellis was white, blue and pink. The trellis itself carried three **clematis (Nelly Moser, Abundance** and **Madame Julia Correvon)**, two **roses (Bobbie James** and **Pink Perpetué)** in front of which were **ceanothus, ceratostigma, choisya, foxgloves, geraniums** (three varieties), **heuchera, Lords** and **Ladies, penstemon, scabious, sedum** and **stachys** – to name but a few!

The colour theme for the end bed in front of the compost area was yellow and bright red – a sharp contrast to the main border. The plants include *Elaeagnus commutata*, orange and red **penstemon**, orange **lily, amelanchier, hollyhocks, schizostylis,** *Hosta fortunei*, **pieris, red roses** and **heuchera**, all backed by **ivy (Gold Heart)** on the fence.

There is also a small, round raised bed by the house where the client can 'cheat' with a succession of buried pots which ensure flowers blooming in all seasons. As a central focal point, there is now a millstone propped up against a big clay vase.

This small garden demonstrates the potential of starting from scratch and how essential it is to plan a total concept. It works well because it is tended by a devoted gardener.

Conclusions

When considering the vital question of where start, the camera is particularly useful. The photographs provided by the client gave me the clue to it all – to concentrate on the sunny area on the right back of the garden and not to attempt to include plants or paving areas which would always be in shade. Plants must have light and water to thrive.

GLEBE FARM COTTAGE
From farmyard to frontispiece

The most noteworthy thing about gardeners is that they are always optimistic, always enterprising, and never satisfied. They always look forward to doing something better than they have ever done before.

Vita Sackville-West

'Before'

The owners of a recently renovated cottage wanted to substitute the surrounding farmyard and outbuildings with a garden. On my initial visit I decided the back of the property needed shelter from the harsh easterly winds, while the northern side required screening from passers-by. A photograph taken before work commenced illustrates the chaotic style fronting the house, consisting of a plain tarmaced yard with various chicken houses and shanty-like corrugated iron buildings in the background.

The farmyard was grossly untidy and overlooked by traffic passing close to the cottage door. There was an absence of cottage flowers and paths; additionally, the property had no clear boundaries and the house was touched by the back lawn which was on a higher level. A new drive would divert vehicles away from the cottage's traditional front walls (stone and brick). Interest could be added by paths of cobblestones, together with some excavation to widen areas close to the rear of the house. Shelter would be established through planting conifers and a pergola of **larch** covered with **roses** on the eastern edge. The barn could be relocated to the south so enclosing the scene yet improving the views from the house.

The cottage is principally 15th century with a wheat thatched roof and brick walls set in a wooden frame (similar to John Constable's *Cottage in a Cornfield,* which hangs in Ipswich Museum). The carriage house is of a later period, probably Victorian, walled with brick and flint, with a slate roof. These two buildings had been conjoined to create a 'gent's res'. Furthermore, there was a small, picturesque staddle-stone granary on the site which could be used in my design. I felt there had never been a more inviting canvas on which to draw a cottage garden.

During renovation, plenty of stone setts in the coach house floor were discovered by the builders and later used for making paths in the

GLEBE FARM COTTAGE

PROBLEMS:
AN UNTIDY FARMYARD WITH VEHICLES PASSING
CLOSE TO FRONT DOOR.
TOO OVERLOOKED BY TRAFFIC. ABSENCE OF COTTAGE FLOWERS.
NO PATHS OR CLEAR BOUNDARIES. BACK LAWN HIGHER THAN
LEVEL OF HOUSE, AND VIRTUALLY ABUTTING THE HOUSE.

SOLUTION:
NEW DRIVE TO TAKE VEHICLES AWAY FROM HOUSE FRONT.
WALLS IN THE VERNACULAR – STONE AND BRICK – PATHS OF
COBBLESTONES. SOME EXCAVATION TO WIDEN AREAS
CLOSE TO REAR OF HOUSE. A PERGOLA OF LARCH
COVERED WITH ROSES. NO MANICURED LAWNS, CONIFERS.

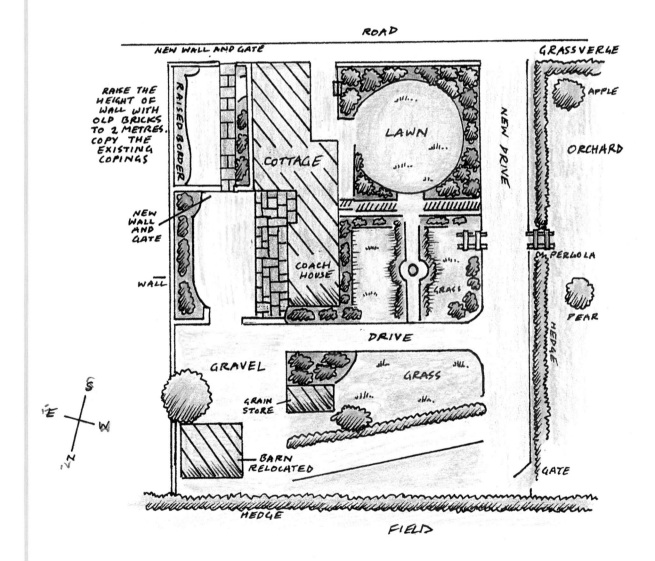

garden; elsewhere, amounts of flint were unearthed and used for constructing garden walls. What the residents needed was privacy, a relocated drive to take vehicles away from the narrow (sunny) front of the house, and some landscaping that enhanced the property and its surroundings.

A formal plan was then drafted taking these strategies into account:

❖ The barn was moved from alongside the house into the southwestern corner and given a blue clock.

❖ Earth was excavated at the back of the house to provide a series of gravel terraces supported by brick walls, which were surrounded with cottage flowers. All were subject to the geometry of the rising stone steps and brick walls up to the lawn above, and were encouraged to grow in unplanned masses. These terraces led to the higher lawn flanked by quick-growing shrubs, including semi-mature **viburnum, berberis, choisya** and **spirea**. A pergola and a row of *Buddleja globosa* gave shelter at the east side by the new driveway.

❖ A simple brick and flint wall was placed at right angles to the house, parallel with the new back drive. A **lavender** walk was created from that part of the drive to the small lawn, with a bird bath centrally placed.

❖ The front garden (previously the entrance drive) was walled up at both ends and iron-gated to create a peaceful structure which harmonised with the cottage's handsome façade.

The whole design was attuned to the cottage environment. The raised bed in the small front garden was filled with a profusion of perennials and grey-leafed herbs **(rosemary, santolina, cistus, echinops, lythrum** etc.) with **aubrietia** and **soapwort (saponaria)** tumbling down the retaining wall. At the back of the house, tiers of **lavender, phlomis** and white **Kent roses** were planted, interspaced with pink **valerian**. Above the front door, a **New Dawn rambling rose** was placed, which has already covered the front porch. For the winter months, **snowdrops, aconites** and *Iris reticulata* were distributed in the lawns.

Conclusions

It is pleasing to note that within a year after work commenced the residents were able to sit in a completely secluded garden. I was very lucky to be able to use natural and regional materials – bricks, flint, iron gates – and the services of a sensitive professional builder. These features gave distinction to the whole garden design. Additionally, there was space for a new drive, well away from the house, that enabled me to 'wrap' the garden around the property.

HEADLAMS

Sleepless nights over a cottage garden

Gardening is a cooperative affair. I am a part of a neighbourhood in which plants, dirt, rocks, and a human family participate collectively in a love affair with the place.

Jim Nollman,
'Why we garden' from *The Sentient Garden*

My Headlams clients owned a beautiful old cottage which had been recently extended to the east. A swimming pool was planned which provided the opportunity to upgrade the garden and match it to the extended house.

When Prime Minister Harold Macmillan was asked what caused his sleepless nights, he replied, 'Events, dear boy, events.' Similarly, frustrating 'events' during April, May and June 2000 prevented my quiet slumber: torrential rain made earth-moving near impossible because the clay's consistency had turned glutinous. The timetable suffered and so did our nerves! We were concerned that a planting season would be lost and costs would escalate. In the event we just made it!

When making alterations to a garden, the sentimental aspects of the property must be considered. Headlams had been owned by the husband's parents. For those who have known and loved a house over the years, change, even when long overdue, is viewed with concern. Consequently, when my report was read by my client he had reservations about suggested changes to his handiwork – the pond, kennel and handcrafted summerhouse. It was important to establish a structure of negotiation with him; this required a disciplined but flexible viewpoint! To his credit, my client expected the highest standards, as evidenced in the agreed construction of the 30-yard (27.4m) wall using bricks, flint and rounded cappings, on the lane side of the house and garden.

There was little by the way of garden immediately surrounding the house, although it had enchanting views across fields. The house extension had been constructed in a manner which left rather angular retaining walls close to the house on the right side. The views from the study were towards a ragged, narrow vegetable patch, with a dilapidated wooden shed in the distance. A lone, unplanted pond (built some time previously) lay to the left. The property's rear view was dominated by a

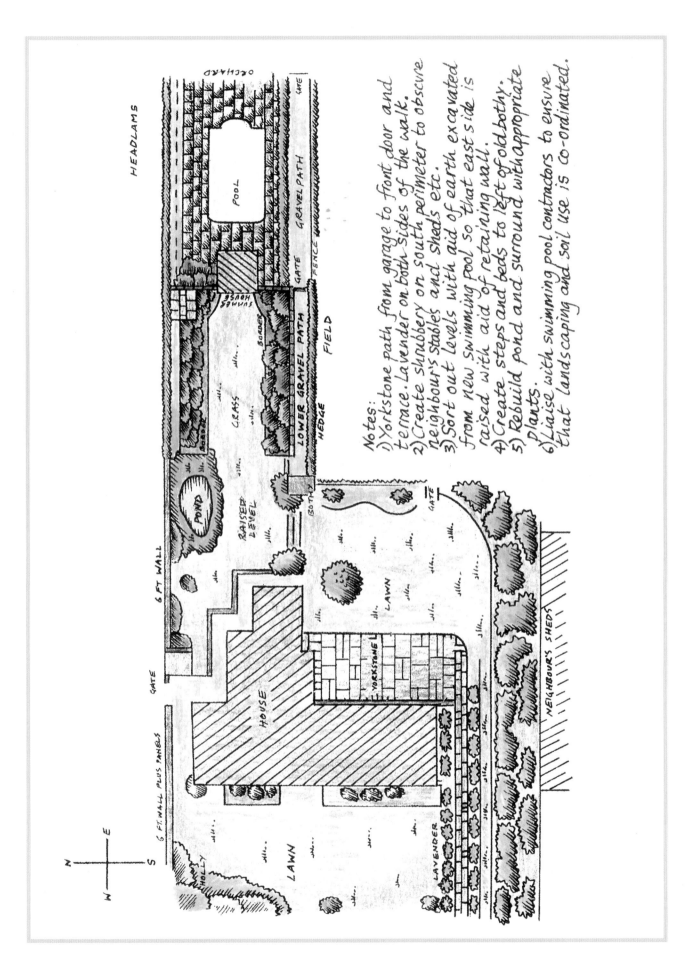

Notes:
1) Yorkstone path from garage to front door and terrace. Lavender on both sides of the walk.
2) Create shrubbery on south perimeter to obscure neighbour's stables and sheds etc.
3) Sort out levels with aid of earth excavated from new swimming pool so that east side is raised with aid of retaining wall.
4) Create steps and beds to left of old bothy.
5) Rebuild pond and surround with appropriate plants.
6) Liaise with swimming pool contractors to ensure that landscaping and soil use is co-ordinated.

tin shed owned by a neighbour, a kennel and some long-expired lilac bushes. The land dropped in all directions except to the east where it rose rather steeply. The plan shows how we made use of the key-shaped plot.

The prospect of digging a new swimming pool promised copious amounts of spare earth for changing levels. The pool area selected was at the higher eastern end of the garden in front of which a pool house and a wall were built to disguise it from the house. **New Dawn roses** and **clematis Perle d'Azur** were also massed in trellis fences at both ends of the swimming pool area, with their pinks and purples lending both striking visual displays and heady scent to an area of relaxation. Dense planting of quick-growing shrubs (notably ***Buddleja globosa*** and ***Cornus alba* Spaethii**) ensured that the tin shed would be obscured from view. Some hedging on the fence line and cottage-type flower borders were planted in various spots. Prominence was given to the lone 'bothy' (probably the original outside loo) and a series of steps and plantings was constructed in order to link it to the new garden. A **lavender** walk from the garage to the front door provides a welcoming feature to those entering the property from the roadway. The principal components of the twin borders were **geraniums** and **procumbent roses**. These were overlapped with **penstemons**, various pink and white plants, and at the back, grey-leafed shrubs – **phlomis**, *Buddleja* **Lochinch**, etc. Around the little pool were planted **ferns, hebes, bamboo, hostas** and other spiky plants, which work with water. Shrubs now obscure the neighbour's sheds.

Post-design photographs taken three months after planting the new borders display how rapidly the garden developed.

34

Conclusions

There are no reminders now of the horrific conditions which made work so long and difficult – eight weeks of unbroken rain! The quality of the soil was even worse than tests initially indicated; a combination of the clay and limestone earth found in Oxfordshire. Consequently, it was only used to raise the garden's foundations; imported loam dressed the lawns and made up the borders. Since completing this task, the adjoining field has been placed on the market – so back we will go!

OLD SCHOOL HOUSE

Redefining the playground

It seemed to my friend that the creation of a landscape-garden offered to the proper muse the most magnificent opportunities. Here indeed was the fairest field for the display of the imagination, in the endless combining of forms of novel beauty.

Edgar Allan Poe

My professional opinion was sought on a property belonging to a newly acquired Victorian village school house. My clients wished to alter the open school-like atmosphere of the grounds to suit the private family house which the building had become. The family had two teenage girls, one a passionate horse-rider, and a younger boy of four. A field and stables had been acquired for the horses and the interior of the house had been updated. The budget allowed little in the way of major landscaping.

Builders of old schools had an instinctive sense of what was right for a teaching environment. The striking Victorian building stands in contrast to the monotonous cube-like structures of modern establishments. It has lovely brick walls, tall windows and a bell tower. The original school room also had a double height ceiling and gallery to the left of the interior. The laughter of children seemed to resonate from the building.

Around the front of the property were the remains of the old playground; several tons of tarmac had been worked into its surface over past years. At the back stood a flat-roofed extension and a conservatory, neither of which fitted harmoniously with the older architecture. There was an uninteresting view of the fields from the drawing room (looking through sliding windows) but a large beech tree to the left stood upon the landscape like a beacon of hope. This project turned out to be a seminal event for my design practice; my clients had a wide circle of friends in south Oxfordshire, many of whom commissioned my services following the successful completion of the garden.

My client's family owned an important garden in the Mendips – in two acres her parents had created the quintessential English garden and I was asked if I could achieve a similar result at the Old School House, albeit on a modest scale! Coincidentally, the late David Hicks, who was a near neighbour, had come up with some ambitious ideas – a lake,

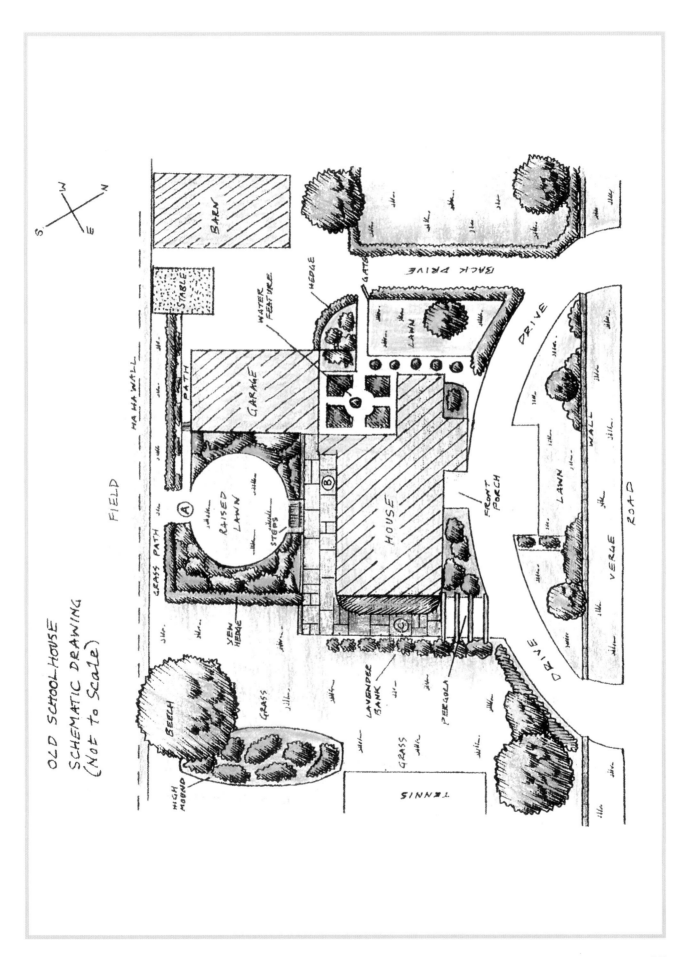

OLD SCHOOLHOUSE
SCHEMATIC DRAWING
(Not to Scale)

sheltered areas with pleached lines surrounding them, and a formal structure around the house moving onto woodland planting beyond. Attractive, but a little grand and too expensive for what my clients had in mind, so we went back to the drawing board.

We collectively agreed that the garden was too open and exposed from all sides. There were no secret places in which children could hide and no surprises for anyone walking around the garden. The direction of the drive through a single gate meant visitors were drawn to the service area of the house rather than to its pretty front porch. (The portico's design was unique and one of the School's gems.) But, if a second entrance gate were to be inserted in the front wall, with a drive passing the door then the mood of that side of the building would be altered positively.

The plan shows how the main features were to be constructed:

❖ On the east side of the house there would be a York stone path linking the new drive to the side of the house with a small pergola over the initial stretch; this path was to proceed further down the side of the house with a **lavender** bed on the left, and **valerian** and climbers on the right.

❖ On the south side I suggested the creation of a wide terrace of natural stone beyond, which would be a raised formal area made by removing earth from areas where levelling was needed (in particular from a ha-ha between the garden and field). Wide stone steps would go up from the terrace.

❖ Into this raised area a circular lawn surrounded by herbaceous beds backed by formal **yew** hedges would be introduced.

❖ On the west side of the house I put a part-parterre garden which would provide an interesting backdrop for the kitchen area and for those coming into the house from the garage. It was to be fenced in to provide a safe haven for children and dogs.

❖ Other features mainly consisted of installing hedges and single specimen shrubs to provide privacy and vertical interest near the tennis court and road.

The last procedure entailed creating a bank of earth (about 20 yards (18.2m), in width and 5 feet (152cm) in height) to the east, which was to be at right angles with the tennis court. The mound was then covered with a selection of evergreen shrubs to enclose the view and enhance the effect of the beech seen from the terrace.

Conclusions

After work had been completed, I met with David Hicks who generally approved of the modest scheme for the Old School House garden. This was a great relief considering his past impressive designs include Broughton Castle (Oxfordshire), Blenheim Palace (Woodstock) and Badminton (Avon), to name but three grand examples. Fortuitously, I later followed him on three other assignments – the Old Rectory at Pyrton, Coates House, Swyncome, and White House Farm (see pages 60–65), where he had done some preliminary work. His style was remorselessly disciplined with a great decisiveness of detail paid to garden planning. His archetypal design signature was a green 'room', flanked by pleached or espaliered nut or fruit trees. His influence is sadly missed.

FISHERMAN'S LODGE

A romantic lodge in Berkshire

The Kiss of sun for pardon,
The song of birds for mirth –
One is nearer God's heart in a garden
Than anywhere else on earth.

Moses Hadas

'Before'

Fisherman's Lodge is a romantic lakeside lodge not far from Newbury. A bridge with an artistic metal balustrade spans its driveway and the house has a delightful portico and front garden. At the rear (south) and the side (west), there were simply lawns surrounded by a high hedge. The new owners were seeking a design for these areas that would require minimal maintenance after completion. They wanted a variety of plants and shrubs to establish an all-summer colour in the borders.

The co-owner of the lodge is a passionate gardener who had moved from a larger establishment in Buckinghamshire. She had brought from her old home a large collection of **hostas, heuchera** and **euphorbias**. One of her first enquiries, which I initially could not answer, involved the most suitable placement of the hostas.

A brief inspection of the area south of the house showed that a view of rolling farmland was obstructed by a 9-foot (274cm) high thorn hedge. This high boundary appeared visually to reduce the area of the enclosed space; a problem solved by introducing a gap in the hedge and also reducing its height. Similarly, planting verticals (trees and hedges) in a line moving away from the house and laying a central stone path down the middle (between parallel borders) would help to give a spacious appearance in this key garden 'room'.

The plan shows a simple design for the garden's southern half:
- ❖ A terraced area to be constructed immediately behind the house.
- ❖ A parterre beyond with **box, lavender, roses**, etc, using York stone for the dividing paths.
- ❖ The rectangular lawn area beyond to incorporate two parallel borders 12 feet (3.6m) wide, into which pink, white and blue herbaceous plants would be introduced.
- ❖ Some specimen **roses** to be placed near the pool.

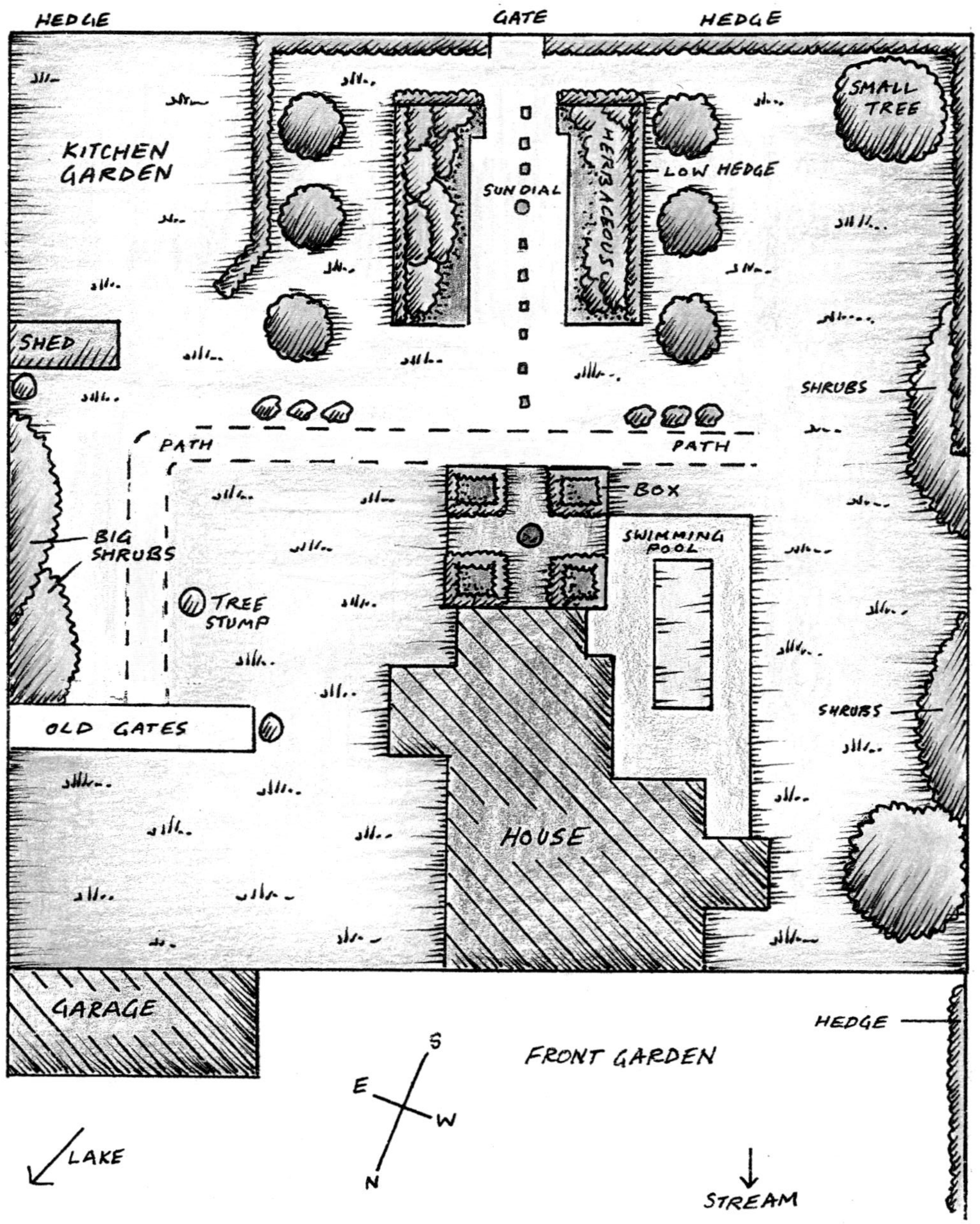

Fisherman's Lodge – South Aspect

Challenges
• No colour or garden structure to rear.
• High hedge blocking view and shortening garden southwards.
• To the east roofs of ugly barns appear when winter removes tree cover.
• Generally featureless on west side.

Solutions
• Parallel herbaceous beds, backed by hedging and enlivened by some shrubs with central lawn radiating from house rear.
• Renew parterre treatment close to house with lavender, roses and box and small terrace.
• Obtain farmers consent to reduce hedge height and insert (false) iron gate at key focal point to south, so lengthening view.
• Plant six rowan trees in line, some specimen rose shrubs and viburnum alongside herbaceous area to breakup the straight lines and give vertical interest.
• Move cornus on west hedge line.
• Yew and hawthorn hedge and trees shielding vegetable garden.

HEDGE

KITCHEN GARDEN

SMALL TREE

HEDGE

LOW HEDGE

SHRUBS

GATE

HERBACEOUS

SUN DIAL

PATH

BOX

SWIMMING POOL

SHRUBS

HEDGE

STREAM

FRONT GARDEN

HOUSE

PATH

TREE STUMP

BIG SHRUBS

SHED

OLD GATES

GARAGE

LAKE

S
E — W
N

To strengthen the effect, three elements were added:

- ❖ A stone path leading through the lawn between the new borders to the (new) iron gate in the hedge.
- ❖ Borderline trees **(Sorbus)** planted parallel to, and behind, the new borders.
- ❖ Hedges planted behind the herbaceous beds to provide visual emphasis and protection from winds.

Finally, with the farmer's consent, a gap was cut through the hedge to create a focal point, which was accentuated by an iron gate and sundial placed in line with the gate and house. On the west side of the house, trees and dogwood were planted to break up the fence line.

Conclusions

The design provided a structural form for the garden which, in the 10 years since the work was completed, the owner has developed, creating a pleasing result. Her parallel borders have excelled; she has taken them in directions of her own and added volumes of pink and white in the front, and planted roses and shrubs such as **Buddleja** **Lochinch** and **berberis** to the rear. Her additions have created one of the great charms at Fisherman's Lodge – the combination of glorious informality at the front of the property with geometric formality to the rear. It was at the front of the house the **hostas** and **hellebores** finally came to rest, while the giant **Christmas rose (Hellebores niger Maximus)** has pride of place in a border close to the stream and bridge.

THE LEAZE

Extending and renovating an established garden

In the creation of a garden, the architect invites the partnership of the Kingdom of Nature. In a beautiful garden the majesty nature is ever present, but it is nature reduced to human proportions and thus transformed into the most efficient haven against the aggressiveness of contemporary life.

Luis Barragán, Mexico

The clients wished for 'a garden worthy of the house' and were prepared to commit to a significant expenditure in order to achieve that end. The setting was ideal – an old cottage-type house at the end of a beautiful common in south Oxfordshire. Much effort was made to echo some of the features seen in other neighbouring gardens on the common and to secure natural materials.

The house had witnessed the growth of a large family – three clever daughters, a very athletic young son and charming parents, who were very excited at the prospect of upgrading the surroundings of their ancient cottage. To the south were six acres of field with tennis courts and a swimming pool dropped in almost at random, and to the west was an orchard, sparse and with huge shrubs and banks of laurel on the fence line, but with no path or pattern. (The photograph is defaced by scribbles – something I do frequently when trying out ideas!) Close to the kitchen on the west side was a delightful old walled garden, secluded and sunny, which was rhomboid rather than rectangular in shape and overtaken by lank grass. At the entrance to this walled enclosure was a huge mound of earth which looked like a Roman tumulus. To the north was an entrance area which had a tall beech hedge and a circular drive which only needed a central bed to make it 'right'.

The measuring of the original garden was quite an experience. I left Edward, an engineering student, with the task, without appreciating how meticulous he would be given his training – a job that would have taken me two or three hours took him two days! Once we had a plan of the site, I discussed the possibilities with the owners. We agreed that the different areas would be well served by using different shapes – a loose form around the swimming pool, a rectangle for the new herbaceous garden, elliptical reshaping of the orchard-cum-shrubbery, and a rather Persian approach to the unusual walled garden alongside the

THE LEAZE GARAGE

POOL HOUSE

E N ——— S W

ENTRANCE

BEECH HEDGE

IRON RAILING

PAVED HOUSE GATE

FIELD

GRAVEL WATER GRASS GATE

OLD WALL

ORCHARD SHED PAVED

GRASS SLOPES WALNUT GATE

SHED

Main Plans
Round off entrance area. Add trees (two
walnuts) and some mature shrubs in informal
area using pergola etc. Screen swimming
pool from house. Create formal garden to
South, with walls on 3 sides and level
lawn. Yorkstone terrace facing formal garden
with an improved verandah. Stone path all
round house, especially wide by kitchen area.
Generally give shape and style to orchard.
Herb and grey plants in eastern garden
create a rectangular effect in rhomboid setting!
Obtain permission for farm gate 200 yards
to the south in line with iron gate.

kitchen. I say 'rather Persian' because it contained a long but overgrown water channel in the centre; it reminded me of gardens in Shiraz and Isphahan with the channels, basin and pavilion, with lattice-work windows placed at the end of the channels. More prosaically, we also determined that a formal pergola barrier should be created between the new herbaceous garden and the existing tennis court and swimming pool area, which loomed rather large when seen from the main rooms of the house.

The rather crude outline of the plan, which brings together the schemes used for the large property, is shown above. The layout of the house was shaped like a boomerang and the existing walls and features to the north were not aligned with that side of the house. It was a question of making the best of existing features and enclosing a formal space to the south which was overlooked by the drawing room. The aim

was to link each zone to the next by means of paths and walks, as well as creating a place for relaxing in the sun.

Much earth-moving was needed to create level areas around the house and to expand the lower terrace in the rhomboid enclosure alongside the kitchen. Dividing walls, built with second-hand bricks and topped with old capping bricks were introduced into the scheme, giving an appearance of maturity. The new pergola, faced with a bold diamond-patterned trellis, gave a gravelled path access from the front garden to the field beyond. It also assisted in obscuring views of the swimming pool area from the new formal garden and from the windows of the sitting room. The trellis was swathed in pale pink *Clematis montana* for spring interest – the leaves of which provided a romantic backdrop for the sprawling bowers of cream and white **roses**, with **nepeta Six Hills Giant** at the ground level lining the gravel path.

Three **walnut** trees were planted, one in the orchard, one in the field near the tennis court, and one beyond the pool area by the garage. These trees were 14 feet (4.2m) high, and the greatest care was taken not to injure any root or fibre. Every layer of root was planted with care and with just sufficient ramming to ensure they stood up unaided. In 20 years time they'll tower like full stops against the blue sky, inviting every young boy who visits to scramble up and hide. I have undertaken the transplanting of fully mature trees – **magnolias, larches, cherries** and **conical hornbeams**. There is no doubt that it may be done with some success, but the cost of transportation and preparation of the ground to receive them is only justified in extreme need for such a feature in a bland landscape (e.g. see Lappingford, page 68).

A very exciting discovery took place during the excavation of the Roman tumulus. After tons of earth were removed, bits of 'greyness' started to emerge. Thinking we were on our way to uncovering a major archaeological discovery, we gingerly picked and blew around the emerging structure. A third of the way in we buried all our hopes of discovering the lost tomb of Akabkhar Hrum, but we were equally thrilled to find … a nuclear shelter! It was known that just after the war this house had been owned by an

American admiral who had naturally determined he should enjoy the greatest degree of safety should there be a nuclear war with Russia. Once the shelter was uncovered we had to think how it could be disguised since there was no question of digging it out. The answer was to design a 'bothy' (hut or shelter) superstructure with a tiled roof and an interesting door to make it look as aged as the wall beside it. It was decided the inside should be turned into a wine cellar – it could have worked equally as well as a teenage drummer's band practice shelter!

Post-design pictures show how the garden looks after two and a half years. The new walled formal herbaceous garden, with a double iron gate leading out onto the field, has quickly matured and the twin beds are planted up with big herbaceous groupings. Tall shrubs have been added at the back to give them quick maturity and to create interest and beauty in the garden without asking for a great deal of maintenance. The walled area close to the kitchen, the rhomboid enclosure, was clearly a very important feature in the whole process of enhancing the gardens. The dominant feature was the crucifix channel to which the paths and planting lines had to be aligned. This area was far from rectangular originally. Low, bushy paths were positioned at the foot of the low wall, beyond the new 'bothy', using plants such as **cistus, santolina, caryopteris** and **rue** in a medley of greys, pink and blues, with just the occasional **procumbent rose** as punctuation.

Conclusions

We all learnt much from this experience. Having previously being disinclined to give time to the garden, the owners have discovered a new love of gardening that will be a source of ever-increasing happiness. For me, it was a chance to change much of the garden, especially the orchard and shrubbery area, in a pictorial way, achieving dramatic effects with the **walnut** tree and some mature **viburnums**. With the aid of a reclamation stockist near Cambridge, I was able to copy some of the styles of neighbouring old cottages (e.g. brick and flint). Sadly the scheme did not run to a Persian garden with damask roses, pomegranates, a pavilion and purifying waterways – but perhaps my clients will reconsider as time goes on!

BIX HILL

A terrace that harmonises with its house

A terrace that harmonises with its house must take its lines from the adjacent building, and must be capacious enough to make the building seem to sit happily within its contours.

Gertrude Jekyll

'Before'

One day in the summer of 1997, a gifted golfing client asked if I would renovate her garden. 'There is too much to look after – the steps are dangerously steep, much is overgrown. Somehow it needs to be given a major facelift.' My first inspection visit showed what lay ahead. The tall white house was approached from a precipitous narrow road; on turning into a rather restricted parking space I saw an attractive garden. There were lots of flower beds, isolated shrubs, mature trees of different kinds, and a spacious lawn falling steeply away from the house on two key sides – the south and west. The jewel of the property was a well-stocked herbaceous garden set into the side of the hill directly below the house, approached by two separate flights of wide handsome (but dilapidated and very steep) stone steps, where four elegant 19th-century classical urns stood on plinths at the top.

The condition of the hillside site suggested some form of terracing was needed near the house, supported by a retaining wall 'capacious enough to make the building seem to sit happily'. A retaining wall can be used in an unlimited number of interesting ways; in this case, by following the gradient in a wide gentle curve, we could link the top lawn to the herbaceous garden border below.

My report with plans summarised my initial impressions:

❖ Except for the 'jewel' border, the planted areas invisible from the house should be mainly turfed over (the costs of upkeep alone argued for this).

❖ The main flight of steps should be removed because they were dangerous; the classical urns could be moved elsewhere.

❖ The parking area to the front of the house needed expanding because it was difficult to turn with more than two cars in the drive. Tidying up with **yew** hedging was needed.

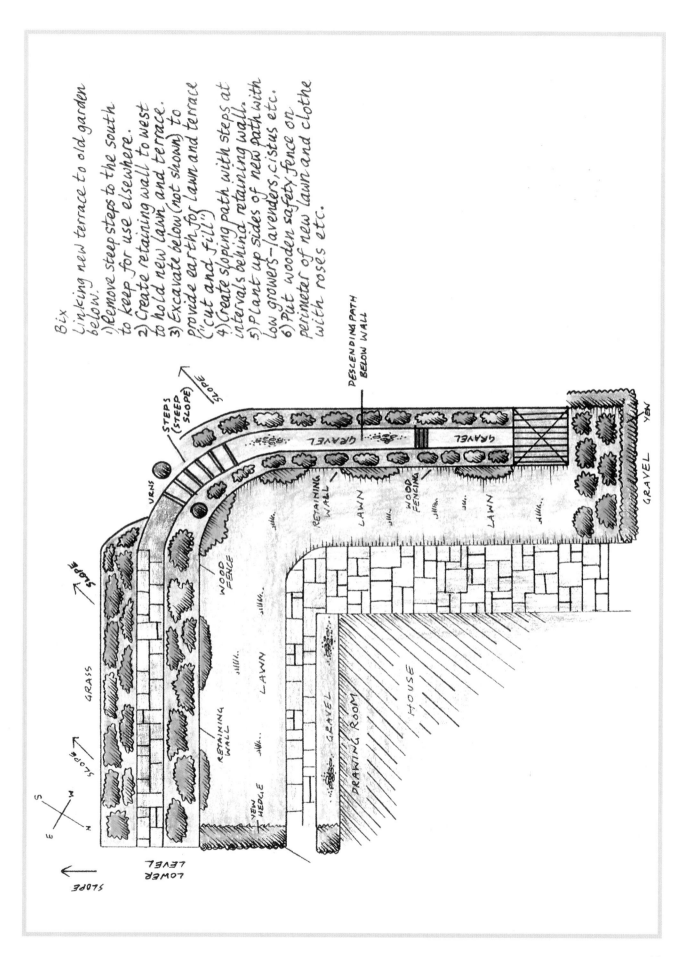

Bix
Linking new terrace to old garden below.
1) Remove steep steps to the south to keep for use elsewhere.
2) Create retaining wall to west to hold new lawn and terrace.
3) Excavate below (not shown) to provide earth for lawn and terrace ("cut and fill")
4) Create sloping path with steps at intervals behind retaining wall.
5) Plant up sides of new path with low growers—lavenders, cistus etc.
6) Put wooden safety fence on perimeter of new lawn and clothe with roses etc.

❖ The key to real improvement lay in providing a level area of lawn around the house, together with a larger York stone terrace beside the house on the south side.

The plan shows how, with the aid of a curving brick retaining wall, a level lawn was created around two sides of the house. A York stone terrace was also laid alongside the building. A pagoda-type pergola, painted green (Sadolin Superdec) placed at the top of the new path serves to provide a focal point from the terrace; it is covered with **New Dawn roses** and **clematis**. Earlier photographs of this site appear to show a massive retaining structure; however, within two years it was transformed, clothed with silver-green foliage and splashes of colour, thanks to the growth of **lavender, caryopteris, cistus, senecio, aubretia, clematis, Perle d'azur** and *Solanum crispum*.

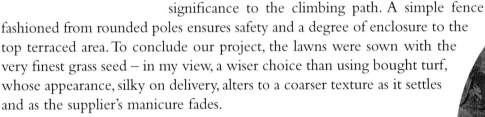

Moving through the garden, one passes down a gentle gradient to where the old herbaceous border, slightly reordered to provide a central path, now flourishes. The overgrown berberis, etc. were removed, leaving room for a marvellous selection of shrubs and herbaceous plants, including a fine collection of **alstroemerias**. Old Victorian urns placed at the base of the new steps, together with the construction of a pergola at their summit, provide an element of significance to the climbing path. A simple fence fashioned from rounded poles ensures safety and a degree of enclosure to the top terraced area. To conclude our project, the lawns were sown with the very finest grass seed – in my view, a wiser choice than using bought turf, whose appearance, silky on delivery, alters to a coarser texture as it settles and as the supplier's manicure fades.

Conclusions

The work at Bix Hill depended heavily on the skill and imagination of the landscaping team. It was not a task where precise plans and instructions could be drawn up – flair and persistence were the watchwords. It was not inexpensive. Landscaping expenditures cannot be precisely accounted in advance as circumstances may add to the work; at Bix Hill for example, we did not collect enough soil from the excavated areas and had to supplement with imported soil. Despite this, the client's enthusiasm for change never faltered.

SELBORNE
A small garden transformed

Laying out grounds may be considered a liberal art, in some sort like poetry and painting.

Wordsworth

The garden at Selborne, a property whose name derived from a type of brick, was an interesting commission. Selborne was owned by a young couple with modern attitudes and perspectives who were not looking to recreate a past era through 'olde worlde' touches. Their house was uncompromisingly up-to-the-present with contemporary additions, white-tiled interior floors, dark walls and large picture windows inside; outside, steel supports for the patio roof, blue back paviours on the terrace and concrete benches and tables placed thereon. Both clients knew their own minds and wanted to be involved in determining how their precious site should be developed.

The house was almost as wide as the plot and the garden was twice as long as its width. There was only room for two themes: an open sunny area close to the house, patio extension and kitchen, and a separate informal region further down the garden, containing a circular pond opposite a small copse of existing fir trees.

I felt an assortment of West Coast and Japanese garden touches was needed to complement the modern house interior. Thus, a combination of **bamboo** blocks, plenty of small **maple** trees, free-growing procumbent plants and a water feature would create overall visual, contemporary harmony. The clients agreed with these plans, and incidentally, so did their young son who took a close interest throughout the project and helped where he could – memories of my days with Bert were frequently jogged!

The garden measured 25 yards (22.8m) across and 55 yards (50.2m) in length. Its prime function had been to give the young family a lawn and garden in which to play. I undertook the task of revising the design and planting in a manner which reflected the contemporary style of the house interior. The original terrace against the house had been built with a mixture of paviours and rounded pebbles brought home from the

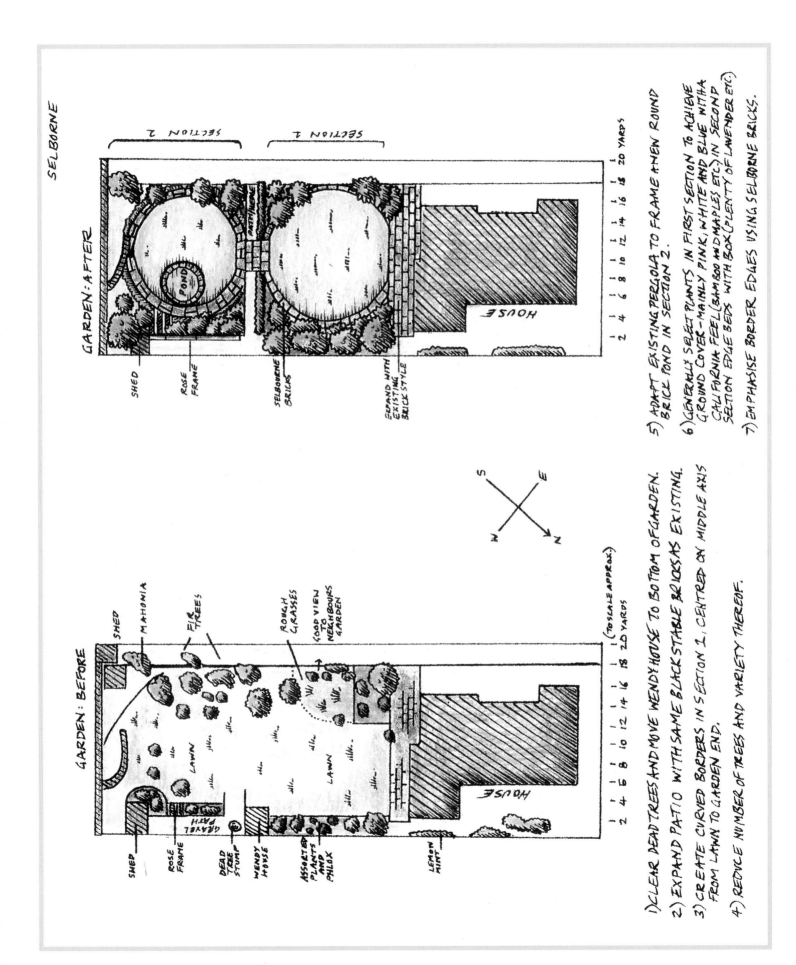

SELBORNE

GARDEN: AFTER

SECTION 2

SECTION 1

SHED

ROSE FRAME

POND

SELBORNE BRICKS

PATH/ARCH

EXPAND WITH EXISTING BRICK STYLE

HOUSE

2   4   6   8   10   12   14   16   18   20 YARDS

5) ADAPT EXISTING PERGOLA TO FRAME A HEN ROUND BRICK POND IN SECTION 2.

6) GENERALLY SELECT PLANTS IN FIRST SECTION TO ACHIEVE GROUND COVER – MAINLY PINK, WHITE AND BLUE WITH A CALIFORNIA FEEL (BAMBOO AND MAPLES ETC.) IN SECOND SECTION EDGE BEDS WITH BOX (PLENTY OF LAVENDER ETC.)

7) EMPHASISE BORDER EDGES USING SELBORNE BRICKS.

S   E   W   N

GARDEN: BEFORE

SHED

MAHONIA

FIR TREES

ROUGH GRASSES

GOOD VIEW TO NEIGHBOURS GARDEN

LAWN

LAWN

SHED

ROSE FRAME

GRAVEL PATH

DEAD TREE STUMP

WENDY HOUSE

ASSORTED PLANTS AND PHLOX

LEMON MINT

HOUSE

(TO SCALE APPROX.)

2   4   6   8   10   12   14   16   18   20 YARDS

1) CLEAR DEAD TREES AND MOVE WENDY HOUSE TO BOTTOM OF GARDEN.

2) EXPAND PATIO WITH SAME BLACK STABLE BRICKS AS EXISTING.

3) CREATE CURVED BORDERS IN SECTION 1, CENTRED ON MIDDLE AXIS FROM LAWN TO GARDEN END.

4) REDUCE NUMBER OF TREES AND VARIETY THEREOF.

53

coast; we decided to dispense with the pebbles and use more bricks to double the area of the terrace overall.

Perhaps the biggest problem was the quantity and variety of trees: eight mature fir trees, two Gingkos, three cherries, a Catalpa, a pagoda tree (*Sophora japonica*), a *Cytissus battandieri*, five small Japanese maples and a weeping pear – all in an area not much bigger than a tennis court! The owner had been a keen collector of unusual tree varieties over the years but she accepted the decimation of her embryonic arboretum with good grace. In the end we majored on the pagoda tree (a relation of Robinia) as a focal point near the centre of the garden. It was also decided that the fir tree copse at the far end should be left as it stood, given that half was in their neighbour's garden!

A border with a low hedge behind was placed halfway down the garden (and traversed by a brick path) separating the two themes. I drew two circles on the preliminary plan so as to concentrate the mind – later repeating this procedure on the grass with 'upside down' spray paint. As the plan shows, the first room contained a circular lawn and a terrace while the second received a sort of parterre treatment, making use of the existing rose pergola in the left back corner of the garden. This maximised the view of plants seen from the back of the house and introduced a sense of mystery (and a focal point) through the new transverse hedge down the central path.

A pool of water was included in the second compartment – partly with the aim of attracting birds, but mainly because my clients, like the Persians, wanted water; they talked of the rhythms and movement in the reflections of the fir trees, the kingfisher flashing its turquoise fire above the pool, and similar poetic notions.

Conclusions

The neighbours' gardens on all three sides could be glimpsed from the terrace, especially in the winter when leaves had fallen, so some care was needed to merge their influence with those in the main garden. The work was done at a time when cloudburst followed cloudburst, causing maximum havoc and ugliness of outlook from the kitchen. It tested the clients' nerve almost to breaking point!

BLENHEIM COTTAGE

Wrapping a garden around an old coaching inn

Gardens are not made by sitting in the shade.

Rudyard Kipling

A design was needed which would wrap a garden around the cottage, create privacy in front and order in other directions. An informal series of rooms had to be developed on the sloping site, along with connecting paths, steps and raised flowerbeds; pergola arches at the top of the main steps would be key components.

The property is located a mile down a narrow, hidden, uneven lane, which at one time had been the main road between London and Oxford. The cottage had been a pub or a small hotel in its heyday, and when I first saw it, it was unfinished and forlorn. My clients were seeking seclusion from 'the jarring world' and looking for garden ideas that would blend harmoniously with the surrounding countryside. At the rear of the house were vestiges of an old terraced garden which were largely removed when the house was remodelled. Gazing up at this garden my eye caught several features which seemed promising – a Ptelea tree (Hop tree) with its aromatic spreading foliage, a good collection of bold paeonies, lots of alstroemerias with their showy multicoloured lance-shaped flowers, and much else besides. The garden needed to be reorganised with some transfers made to other areas so that a good foundation could be created to build up consistent groupings to the back and sides of the house. There was a major box bush to the side which could be worked into the design. In the front there was little vegetation and no distinction between road and front garden.

In my report (later supplemented by other reports) I concluded that for the garden design to be effective it would have to encompass the whole area surrounding the house, involving the creation of an integrated and harmonious setting. The walks, paths and steps had to be reconstructed on a generous scale. In musical terms (reflecting its musician owner), the garden needed a melodic composition with imaginative phrasing. The score suggested included some fortissimo

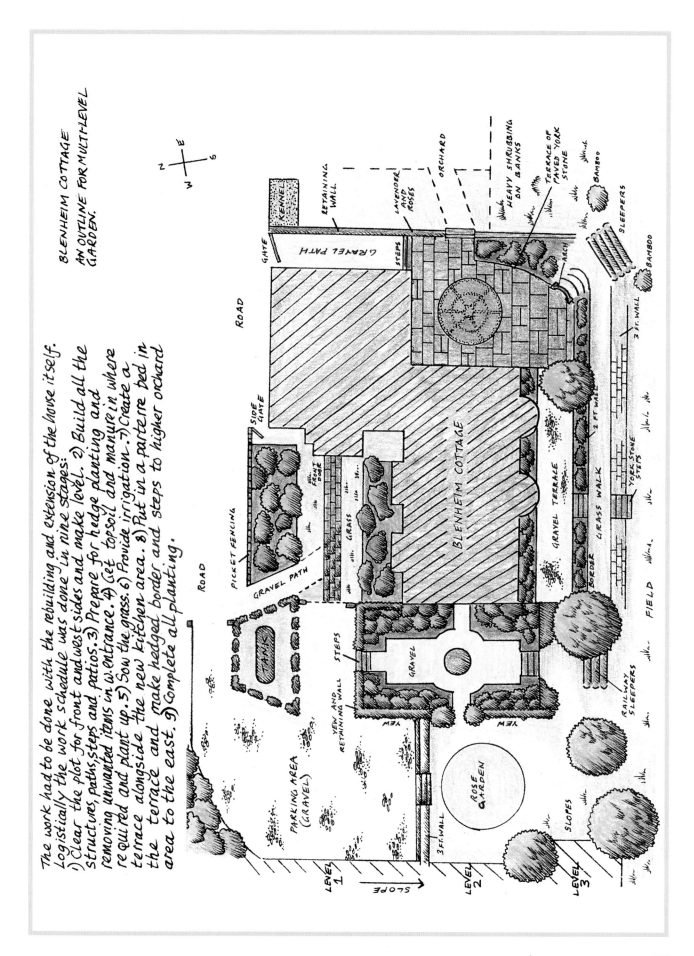

BLENHEIM COTTAGE

AN OUTLINE FOR MULTI-LEVEL GARDEN.

The work had to be done with the rebuilding and extension of the house itself. Logistically the work schedule was done in nine stages:
1) Clear the plot for front and west sides and make level. 2) Build all the structures, paths, steps and patios. 3) Prepare for hedge planting and removing unwanted items in w. entrance. 4) Get topsoil and manure in where required and plant up. 5) Sow the grass. 6) Provide irrigation. 7) Create a terrace alongside the new kitchen area. 8) Put in a parterre bed in the terrace and make hedged border and steps to higher orchard area to the east. 9) Complete all planting.

plantings at the top of the walks and at the corners, allowing for an andante stroll along the lower paths; tranquillo phrasings were to be used for the terraces against the house. Any streptiso or boisterous elements were to be regulated to the shrubbery. The owners had no wish to garden seven days a week which meant reducing some existing parts of the garden as well as creating new ones. There was a great deal of levelling to be done; new dry retaining walls at the back of the house had to be created and the majority of the steps leading from the field up to the top terrace at the back of the house had to be rebuilt and re-sited. During this development period the builders had yet to complete certain parts of the house, such as the kitchen and front entrance, so we were asked to proceed poco a poco.

The plan conveys how the zones were linked to each other and the way the descending levels were devised with a mixture of formal and informal shapings. Two Victorian rose arches were employed to provide the vertical fortissimos at the top of the steps – one at the western entrance and one at the far end of the gravel walk on the return to the main terrace by the kitchen.

The front of the property had previously been used for car parking and it was agreed the area should be fenced off to prevent people parking there. I envisaged that the front borders against the road would contain certain cottage-type plants and shrubs of all-year-round interest at the back which would grow to a reasonable height to obscure a clear view of the front door from the street.

As a part of a series of linked walkways, a gravel walk was built in the south side, midway between the (low) field and upper terrace surrounding the house. We did not want to do a wholesale rebuilding job; this walk had to be manoeuvred because it was narrower at one end, a fault disguised with the aid of some **lavender** planting at the wider end.

In the autumn we returned to photograph the site. The gravel was down and the flowers were open. A score which had started with a vague set of rhythms had been transposed into an acceptable composition – the quaver/semi-quaver patterns were correctly grouped and the right octave chosen. Sometimes solutions can be seen at a glance, but here one or two features had to be sought and made the basis on which to build the rest.

The west side of the house was transformed by the creation of a parterre-style walkway which was first levelled and then given bold stone steps at the top, bottom and middle.

Conclusions

All major garden projects seem to experience dramatic moments. Nearing the end of the first phase in this project only the patch below the garage area remained to be tilled and turned into a rose garden. A spirit of optimism reigned. The clients were chirpy and the landscaping team was uplifted by a spell of good weather and the prospect of a change of scene. Then disaster struck. Martin Bennett, our trusted and careful team leader, had somehow managed to get his right foot and ankle caught in the tilling machine. A shriek of pain rent the air and we all raced to the spot where he was transfixed. Fortunately, the fire brigade managed to release him and he was fit again within six weeks, but I suspect it was this experience which led this gifted craftsman to abandon landscaping in favour of a new career.

WHITE HOUSE FARM

A Provencal 'mas' in Oxfordshire

And when your back stops aching and your hands begin to harden …You will find yourself a partner in the Glory of the Garden.

Rudyard Kipling

A swimming pool is a common catalyst for change. The wish to disguise its impact, the extra soil it produces and the rectangular nature of its outline — all combine to face the owner with major choices. It helps to have experienced advice but do not look to the pool construction company for this. Be wary of those whose motto is 'Dig quickly, pave fast, site close to electricity, exit pronto, take profit.'

The house is approached down a long country road over unseen humps. Then a large house comes into view, with deep roofs, tall chimneys, massive walls of stone and a doorway worthy of a 'mas' in Provence.

The owners had recently moved in with their five sons. Their gardener was a young Dirk Bogarde-like character (from *The Servant*). The leather gloves and his immaculate turnout suggested he would be of greater use pruning roses than shifting earth — indeed, his principal role seemed to be to amuse the children.

The interior of the house is stunning with a huge hall and charmingly decorated. The back faces west — dining room, kitchen and playroom windows looked out on a grassy but empty expanse with a privet hedge slightly askew to the side on the left, and a huge 8-foot (243cm) wall on the right, which would have done justice to a reform school. The drawing room window, facing southeast, looked out on an empty courtyard. It cried out for a parterre-type treatment. The front garden (designed by the late David Hicks) included a splendid drive, many trees and generally needed only minor enhancement.

The clients gave me wide terms of reference: 'You have a lovely garden yourself, please do something similar for us. Put in a swimming pool which is invisible from the house! And don't forget the children's Wendy house is to be given pride of place, not hidden away where it can't be seen from the playroom window.' The plan proposed:

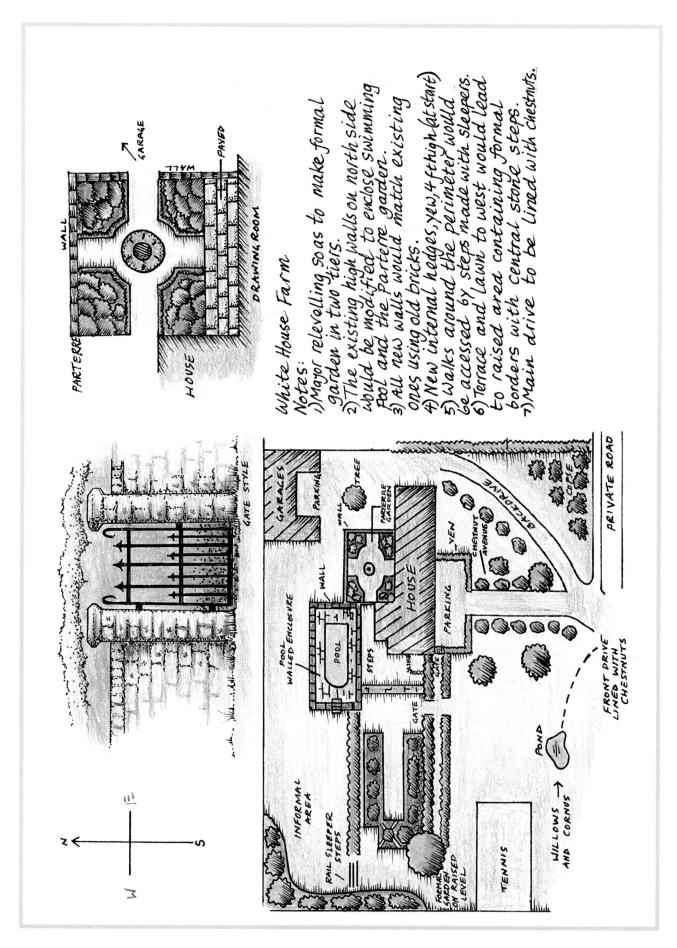

White House Farm

Notes:
1) Major relevelling so as to make formal garden in two tiers.
2) The existing high walls on north side would be modified to enclose swimming pool and the Parterre garden.
3) All new walls would match existing ones using old bricks.
4) New internal hedges, yew, 4 ft high (at start)
5) Walks around the perimeter would be accessed by steps made with sleepers.
6) Terrace and lawn to west would lead to raised area containing formal borders with central stone steps.
7) Main drive to be lined with chestnuts.

❖ Terracing the west side with York riven stone against the house.

❖ Providing added interest by creating two levels in the back garden (the excavation of the pool and first part of the old lawned area would provide the necessary means of achieving this).

❖ Planting a second hedge (of **yew**) on the left side inside the line of the (slightly askew) privet, so symmetry could be achieved in the formal herbaceous area.

❖ Constructing the pool in a 'room,' surrounded by a **yew** hedge to the south and east, by the existing wall to the north (first reduced by 2½ft/76.2cm) and to the west by the pool house with walling to match existing types elsewhere.

❖ Terracing the area outside the dining room with York stone surrounded by a double hedge of **Hidcote lavender**, inside which were to be planted **Kent (white) repeat flowering roses**.

❖ Sundry changes to wall borders and herbaceous borders, to create a shrubbery behind the pool house and generally to achieve progression around the whole property by paths and walks.

❖ Giving the enclosed walled garden around the drawing room 'parterre' treatment, with **box** hedging, massed herbs and an old sundial in the centre of the crossing gravel paths.

❖ Extending the avenue of **chestnuts** down the drive at the front of the house and planting a **yew** hedge around the parking area.

❖ Putting a square pergola with roof trusses as a central focal point at the west end, painted Sadolin Superdec Green.

The photographs show these changes. Wide railway sleeper steps down the back garden lead to the shrubbed area and are accompanied by a bank of **euphorbias** (page 63). The substantial pergola arch at the end of the formal garden, where one can turn left or right is a useful vertical element in the scene – the old apple tree in the left corner being retained. (Beyond the pergola there was potential for a large statue to be installed centrally but this was left as a future possibility.)

The herbaceous borders, planted with shrubs at the back, and pink, blue and white perennials with herbs in the front, proved effective from the start, although rabbits took their toll until netting was installed.

Conclusions

This task went very smoothly thanks to a skilled team and understanding clients, who showed faith in all our endeavours. They never complained about the massive pyramid of earth outside the kitchen window accumulated from all the excavations, which remained for two monsoon-like months until the weather improved!

On the first visit, all the best gardens reveal their individualistic distinctions. The initial view down the drive (for which I was not really the author) had already achieved this. On reflection, I feel the rest has now come some way to match it.

LAPPINGFORD FARM

Acres to spare

Gardeners, I think, dream bigger dreams than Emperors.

Mary Cantwell

'Before'

'After'

This house, with four acres of fields, water and woodland, offered plenty of scope. The new owners had taken me to see the property when it was under offer. One of its many charms was a view of the old village church seen from its entrance. To the south in the distance was a long line of domed hornbeams which separated the garden from farmland beyond. The owners had revolutionised the interior of the house. It was a scintillating success – the more so since they opened up so many views to the south over the planned garden.

The clients showed me photographs of their previous house (in Johannesburg) surrounded by beautiful gardens and asked if I would do something like it swiftly. Upkeep costs should be minimised and the areas adjoining the house, particularly the terraces, should be the main focus of attention. The property was surrounded by rural countryside, with superb views to the south and west. The appearance of the house needed to be softened by romantic planting. The front gravelled area required a circular bed to bring a sense of discipline to the parking plus some adornment by the entrance gate and a vegetable patch needed to be installed to the north. Additionally, hedge lines (with iron arch) were to be constructed further away from the house to make an obvious transition between the formal and informal areas ('the veldt' as we termed it) in this magnificent setting.

The plan shows how the scheme was presented to the client.

Luckily there was a raised grass terrace already edged with stone walls on the south side of the house. Borders were made against the stone edging and excavated to a width of 6 feet (182cm). These were filled mainly with **herbs, cistus, roses** and the like, with limited colours – white, blue and pink. At the corners rather high shrubs, like creamy **rhamnus**, were introduced to emphasise contours.

The terrace itself was paved with York stone with a knot garden

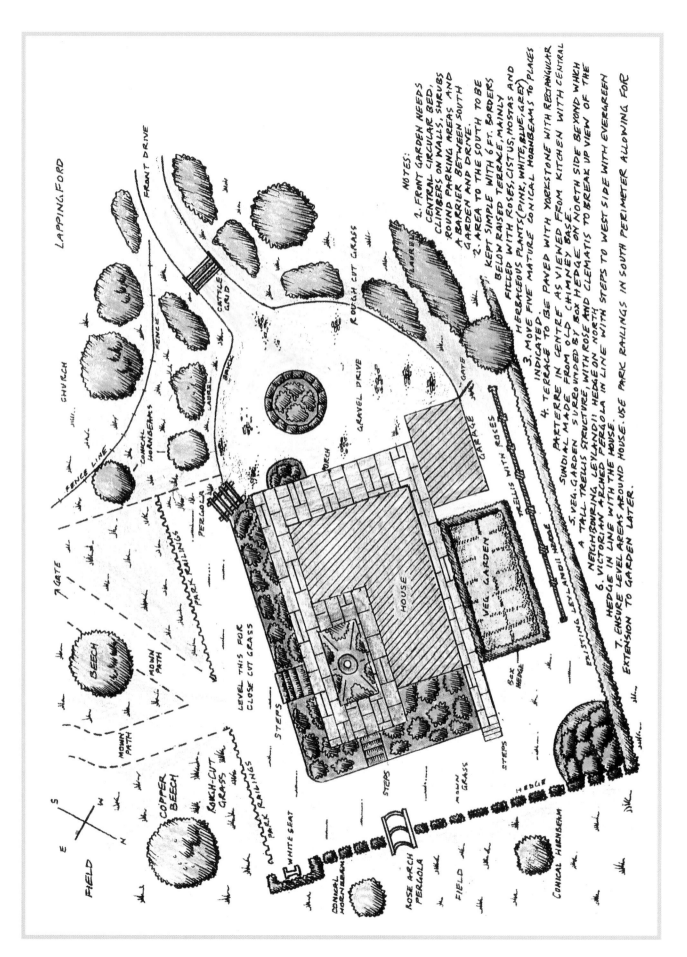

placed in its middle, an old chimney pot at its centre with a sundial stuck to its top livened up the aspect as seen from the hall and kitchen.

The area chosen for the vegetable garden was overlooked by the kitchen and dining room. Consequently, it was important to give it a sense of style as well as utility. We backed the garden with a trellis smothered with pink **clematis** and with clipped **rosemary** at its base – our main aim being to obscure the line of Leylandii on the fence line on that side. **Box** hedging and a sundial also added symmetry.

The planting of several mature trees (including transferring three mature conical **hornbeams**), a hedge and a Victorian arch, gave some vertical barriers through which the lovely 'veldt' beyond could be seen. Near the walls **espalier pears** were combined with cream and yellow **climbing roses**.

Conclusions

What began as another bland site has been much enlivened by the changes. Since completing my task at Lappingford, my client's ambitions for her garden plans have increased. The time has come when many new facets are being added to what is already a satisfying composition.

HILLS HOUSE

Minor embellishment of a manor garden

The garden, full of great delight, its master doth allure.

Nicholas Grimald, 'The Garden'

'I'm determined to remodel the garden before the BBC comes to film it.' Sir John Mills CBE is a model for us all, as forward-looking in his 90s as he was 40 years ago – fit, full of fun, adoring things of beauty, and a great companion. He sought my assistance urgently in the winter of 1996 before the TV crew arrived to interview him in his summer garden. He wanted refreshed borders, tidier path lines, a new terrace, changed rose beds …

Hills House resides in the charming and historical village of Denham, famous for its association with early film-making. The house borders the churchyard and has its own gate to the grounds. It was an enticing experience renovating an old garden about 200 years old – a garden with beautiful walls, walnuts, Indian bean trees and a superb general structure. A feature of particular interest is a gravel path sweeping from the middle of the back of the house, starting at 90 degrees and going off at an angle after roughly 40 yards – a rather effective way of planning the garden – leading you through a walled structure to the orchard and swimming pool beyond. The path is backed by a sturdy brick wall with borders on both sides. This feature, above all others, breaks the rectangular mould in an effective way and provides the chance to display **azaleas** and **acers** in a stunning situation half hidden from the house.

Sir John was keen to accentuate the charm of his already glorious garden despite the fact that due to his failing eyesight the most he would be able to make out would be contours and shadows. I have previously stressed the importance of good 'bone structure' in the garden; Hills House defined this quality, showing a strong basic plan married to the 'profusion and exuberance' which Vita Sackville-West loved.

Sir John was always at hand to encourage. He would frequently be seated at a grand piano in the drawing room, his dog Hamlet lying at his feet, but not really playing with any concentration – he was always ready

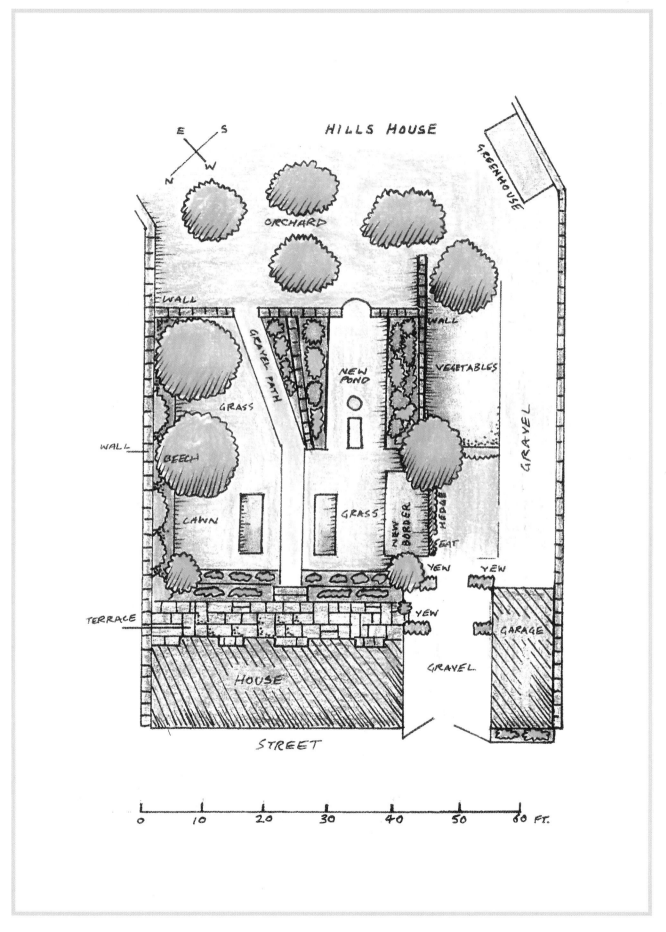

to react when I entered the room. He is not old, more akin to a schoolboy in his enthusiasms. His wife Mary is frail and forgetful, but has her garden very much at heart. She is known for her pithy sense of humour, at its pithiest when discussing Eric, part-time gardener and part-time gravedigger – she opined that he was 'better fitted for deep digging than pruning roses!'

In the sketch of the plan of Sir John's 3-acre garden can be seen the brick walls – 7 feet (213cm) high and three bricks thick in places – that feature prominently and widely, both on the boundaries and within the formal area. Brick walls are a godsend for a designer, enclosing the view, defining the shape and providing an opportunity to manipulate the perspectives through which the garden is seen. The property's soil was neutral, so **rhododendrons, azaleas** and **heathers** flourished alongside the angled wall.

My notes indicated the need to:

❖ Substitute York stone for gravel on the terrace by the house with box hedging by the steps. Sir John had seen and approved of our stone terraces and he was becoming increasingly annoyed by the quantity of stones taken into the house by dog and human feet.
❖ Create an herbaceous bed down the west side. Too little colour could be seen from the house or the terrace – this addition would remedy the problem.
❖ Rearrange the rose borders near the house with the planting of **lavender** edging and the substitution of repeaters like **Kent** and **Sussex County roses**.
❖ Introduce herbs, especially **thyme** and other low growers, in the rather hot and shallow border adjoining the rear of the house. Previously annuals had featured in this border but they had struggled to survive.

Conclusions

The work was carried out partly by my own team (who were enthralled by their close associations with 'a real film star' not forgetting the occasional sightings of his pretty daughters, Hayley and Juliet) and the lugubrious Eric. I'm pleased to report that Eric supported the changes wholeheartedly – not one of the old school! Like Sir John, he shared the view that even the best of old gardens need and benefit from rejuvenating revisions. Sir John recently sold Hills House but as he has moved close by he can keep in touch with his previous garden.

THE PRIORY

Mission: Upgrading the Garden in a Hurry

There is no 'The End' to be written, neither can you, like an architect, engrave in stone the day the garden was finished; a painter can frame his picture, a composer notate his coda, but a garden is always on the move.

Mirabel Osler

Picturesque old garden walls are cherished possessions and when built to enclose a rectangular garden they acquire even more allure. They provide a tremendous run of vertical space on which to grow roses or fruit; they provide a framework (and shelter) into which borders, trees and alleys, can be arranged – preferably symmetrically (since the boundaries are such) and all this without having to think too much about coping with the transition to the world beyond. The Priory offered just such a treat!

An impending wedding had prompted the owners to look around their ancient garden and decide that it demanded a makeover. Neither of the owners were active gardeners – they were too busy with their careers (as a City surveyor and a kitchen designer) and their three children. They relied on their part-time gardener whom they had inherited on acquiring the house. He was from the orthodox school, viewing recommendations for change with suspicion (but he came round later).

The initial meeting with the clients included a visit to all the upstairs rooms and downstairs rooms facing the garden. From this perspective it was clear that worthwhile improvement would follow if greater symmetry was achieved in the layout of the borders and lawn. There was a rather enticing grotto at the far end of the walled garden which probably predated the walling of the area. It was in a state of disrepair and off-centre of the main lawn; greater prominence to this feature was called for. There were other lesser matters which also called for attention such as pruning, and the tying up and training of the superb climbing roses on the 9-foot (274cm) wall to the east side of the garden – these roses would yield an abundance of the most ornamental class of bloom for the wedding ahead.

The entrance to the back garden was down a stone path through an exceptional iron gate. I noted this area needed some evergreen planting

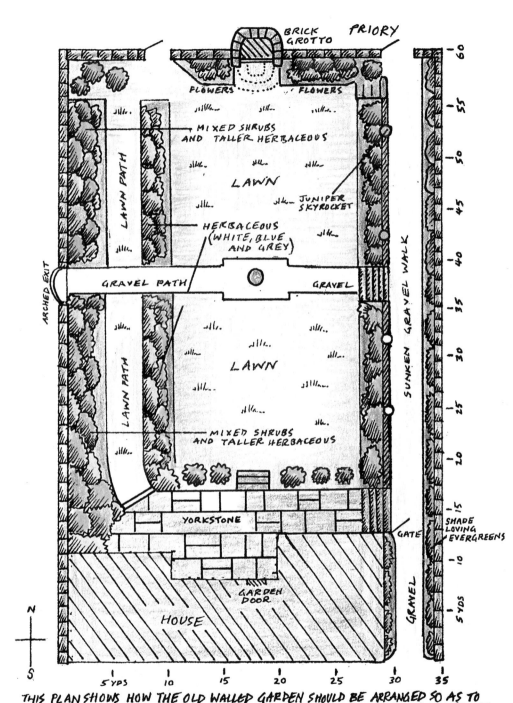

THIS PLAN SHOWS HOW THE OLD WALLED GARDEN SHOULD BE ARRANGED SO AS TO
CENTRE THE LINE OF THE MAIN LAWN ON THE GROTTO-LIKE BRICK SUMMERHOUSE.
NOTES:1) MAKE A SYMMETRICAL LAWN FOCUSED ON GROTTO, CREATING
HERBACEOUS BORDER ON THE LEFT, THE FULL LENGTH OF GARDEN, TO ACHIEVE 'BALANCE'.
2) PUT GRASS PATH BEHIND NEW BORDER WITH NARROW BORDER TO LEFT AGAINST
WEST WALL. 3) EXTEND TERRACE ALONGSIDE HOUSE AND SORT OUT ADJOINING
ROSE BEDS: HEDGE WIDTH. 4) RETRAIN ALL CLIMBING ROSES ON LOWER WALK
EAST SIDE. 5) USE JUNIPER SKYROCKET ON LEFT AND CEANOTHUS ON RIGHT AS
BUTTRESSES TO EMPHASISE LENGTH OF LOWER WALK. 6) GENERALLY REVISE THE
PLANTING AT GATE APPROACH AND NEW HERBACEOUS BEDS AND BEDS BY GROTTO.

on its left side to draw attention away from rather ugly drainpipes; the appearance of the stone arch would improve with some sort of creeper, such as climbing **hydrangea**; and beyond the arch, where there was a sunken path down the side of the walled garden, the rather bare wall on the right would benefit from some adornment such as the planting of upright **ceanothus** at intervals to act as a topiary buttress.

The plan shows how we sought to achieve a more symmetrical treatment of the main lawn by centring it on the lovely grotto. Balance and proportion were achieved among other things by creating a large herbaceous border down the left-hand side. On the lower pathway, which can be seen from the entrance arch, the left-hand dry wall was planted up with a harmonious assembly of plants; a row of **junipers (Skyrocket)** was also planted down that side. On the right against the tall boundary wall, a series of **ceanothus (Blue Spires)**, which give a brilliant blue flower in the right season, also provided the vertical/structural role needed. These features made this route to the far gate seem longer, more important and inviting.

The final planting was done with the immediacy of the wedding in mind – romantic blues and pinks, bushy white masses of **gypsophila (Bristol Fairy)**, lush scented groupings of **Felicia roses**, and vigorous masses of *Viola cornuta* and **artemisias**, all chosen to provide a spectacular show both on the day itself and in the future.

Conclusions

Other consequential changes included the removal of certain inappropriate evergreen trees and bushes close to the house. I would have liked to have done more with the grotto/gazebo itself; its eccentricity is an endearing trait and it combines tranquillity with a southern aspect. But not unnaturally, the owners were apprehensive about the approaching wedding, fearing that their garden would not be finished on time – they need not have worried!

GOLF CLUB
A Terrace in Front of the Golf Club

On a fine day in the spring, summer or early autumn, there are few spots more delightful than the terrace in front of our golf club. It is a vantage point peculiarly fitted to the man of philosophic mind: for from it may be seen that varied and never ending pageant which men call golf in a number of its aspects. To your right on your first tee stand the cheery optimists who are about to make their opening drive, happily conscious that even a topped shot would trickle a measurable distance down the hill. At your side is the eighteenth green with its sinuous undulations which have so often wrecked the returning traveller in sight of home.

P.G. Wodehouse
'A Woman is only a Woman'

Building a garden and terrace for a golf club membership poses special problems. The terrace must be able to accommodate all the people looking for relaxation on a fine summer's day, it must brave close scrutiny in all seasons and weathers and upkeep should be trouble free.

The job was not without its political dimension – the secretary was a charming ex-army officer whose aim in life was to keep the committee happy and the members from complaining. I conjectured that half the members were keen gardeners, the other half keen designers. The plan shows the problems and proposed solutions.

As P.G. Wodehouse stated in *The Long Hole*: 'It is a curious trait of the human mind that however little personal interest one may have in the result, it is more impossible to prevent oneself taking sides in any event of a competitive nature.' This notion may be applied to the supporting and opposing argument about the problematic wall around the terrace on which the members sat. I had removed it, disliking the bricks and grudging the amount of space it took up. It was not long before some of the older members pleaded for the wall to be restored: 'This is what we always sat on; this is what we always put our beer mugs on; we miss the informality of it all.' They won their case!

The photographs show how the beds looked after eighteen months; on one side of the terrace lots of low-growers, **stachys, santolina, phlomis, lavender** and **rosemary**, enlivened by ground cover roses, **Pink Bells shrub rose, rhus**, some dark green **cistus**, etc. In the shaded area we planted more **cistus** plus **euphorbias, hellebores** and **viburnums**.

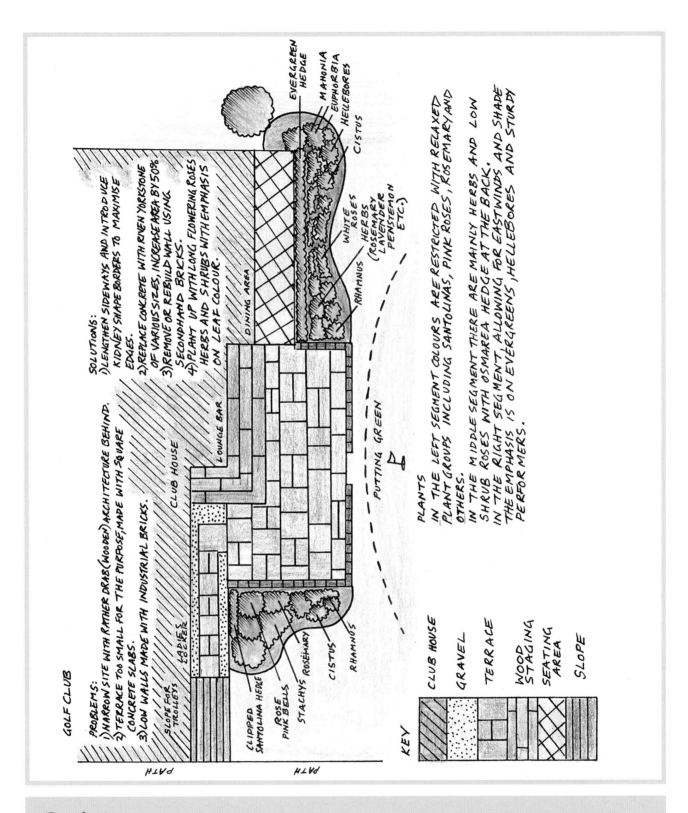

GOLF CLUB

PROBLEMS:
1) NARROW SITE WITH RATHER DRAB (WOODEN) ARCHITECTURE BEHIND.
2) TERRACE TOO SMALL FOR THE PURPOSE, MADE WITH SQUARE CONCRETE SLABS.
3) LOW WALLS MADE WITH INDUSTRIAL BRICKS.

SOLUTIONS:
1) LENGTHEN SIDEWAYS AND INTRODUCE KIDNEY SHAPE BORDERS TO MAXIMISE EDGES.
2) REPLACE CONCRETE WITH RIVEN YORKSTONE OF VARIOUS SIZES, INCREASE AREA BY 50%
3) REMOVE OR REBUILD WALL USING SECONDHAND BRICKS.
4) PLANT UP WITH LONG FLOWERING ROSES HERBS AND SHRUBS WITH EMPHASIS ON LEAF COLOUR.

PLANTS
IN THE LEFT SEGMENT COLOURS ARE RESTRICTED WITH RELAXED PLANT GROUPS INCLUDING SANTOLINAS, PINK ROSES, ROSEMARY AND OTHERS.
IN THE MIDDLE SEGMENT THERE ARE MAINLY HERBS AND LOW SHRUB ROSES WITH OSMAREA HEDGE AT THE BACK.
IN THE RIGHT SEGMENT ALLOWING FOR EASTWINDS AND SHADE THE EMPHASIS IS ON EVERGREENS, HELLEBORES AND STURDY PERFORMERS.

EVERGREEN HEDGE
MAHONIA
EUPHORBIA
HELLEBORES
CISTUS
WHITE ROSES
HERBS (ROSEMARY LAVENDER PENSTEMON ETC.)
RHAMNUS

DINING AREA
CLUB HOUSE
LOUNGE BAR
SLOPE FOR TROLLEYS
LADIES LOCKER
PUTTING GREEN
PATH
PATH

CLIPPED SANTOLINA HEDGE
ROSE PINK BELLS
STACHYS ROSEMARY
CISTUS
RHAMNUS

KEY
CLUB HOUSE
GRAVEL
TERRACE
WOOD STAGING
SEATING AREA
SLOPE

Conclusions

It was truly astonishing how many varieties of foliage could be produced in the confined space, ranging from vivid spring green and gold through to smoky blue, maroon and plum purple in summer, with silver grey all year round. As the secretary said: 'It is never dull to look at' ... an acceptable epitaph!

79

II

CHAPTER II

Lessons Learned: Elements of Garden Making

A garden is a grand teacher.
It teaches patience and careful watchfulness; it teaches industry and thrift;
above all it teaches entire trust.
Gertrude Jekyll

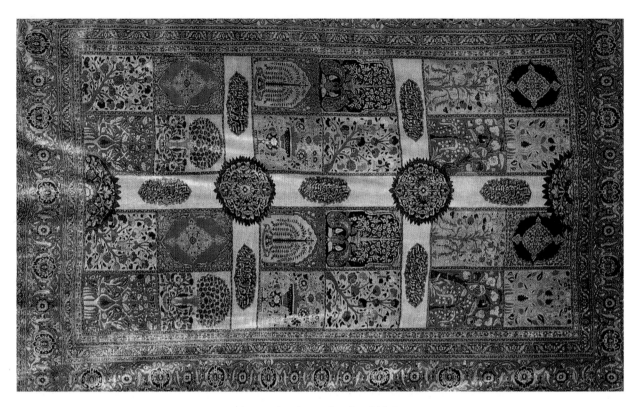

(A) This is the theme for the Old Rectory.

(B) This is the style used for the lawn of White House Farm as well as several other case studies in this book.

(C) This design echoes the parterre in the Old School House.

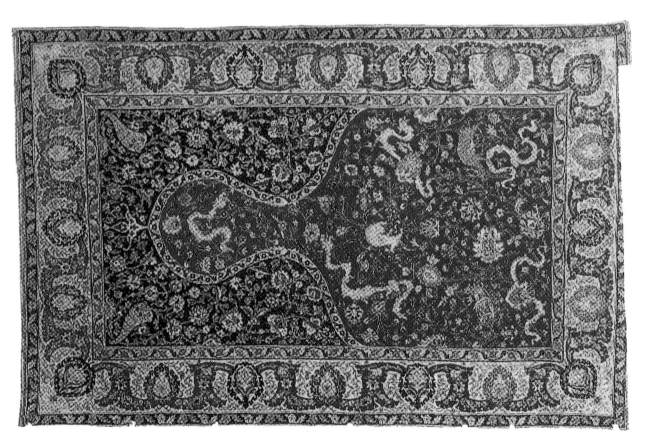

(D) This offers ideas for a secret garden beyond the main lawn area, perhaps with a walk around the perimeter.

What makes for a good design?

Good design benefits everyone: it will add to the enjoyment of the resident, his visitors and the neighbours. It will provide a basis for further development and for the maturing process. Conclusively, it should add significantly to the value of the property.

What elements make for a good design? This question has determined the structure of this book. I have led the reader through 17 experiences of laying out gardens, each to suit the personality of the owner(s), and pinpointed the lessons which emerged from these sometimes daunting experiences.

When I told an American friend I was writing this book, he said, 'It would be good if you could lay down some timeless rules about what makes for a good design.' It set me back on my heels! By now you will know that I am a reverent disciple of Gertrude Jekyll and am the proud owner of many books showing the number of plans she drew up in her long life. It is clear she had a great respect for the architectural profession and worked on many tasks with the respected architect, Edwin Lutyens. Consequently, this raises the question of what an architect would regard as a good design.

The aim of classical architecture is to achieve a demonstrable harmony of the parts which make up the whole. This enables the ratios of all the parts in the building to be related to each other in a direct way. However, when translated into the garden vernacular, the architectural concept of *proportion* is likewise paramount. Certainly, symmetry of design, abundance of planting, elegant sweeps and the matching of the garden to house were Gertrude Jekyll's aims. I believe her designs were not swayed by fashions and that her ideas are still valid today.

It is because one seeks symmetry and proportion in designs that a grid is used (usually graph paper or computerised equivalent) as the basis for producing a plan for a greenfield site. This grid can be simple lines and squares as in graph paper, or it can be a series of circles or diamonds if this fits the situation better. Some degree of symmetry and proportion is more easily achieved with the aid of a site plan.

Gardens have their roots in antiquity, in the worlds of China, Japan and Persia, and later in those of Italy and France. Initially they were intended mainly to complement good architecture, so scale and form were paramount. More recently they have derived much from the tradition of the cottage garden where less attention is paid to scale and form and more to colour, utility and sheer abundance.

It can sometimes help to think about classical shapes such as the floor plan of a church or a Persian carpet design when faced with a greenfield site. In the four photographs of Persian prayer rugs (pages 82 and 83) can be seen the distinctive themes which could be said to have been repeated in some of the gardens described in this book. In short, there is a close proximity of design between gardens and the structure of prayer rugs, some of which display a continuation of centuries-old tradition in an Ottoman Court style.

No plan – no hope

Each case study includes a plan of what has been done – in some cases a simplified one for ease of assimilation. First I draw up an initial plan of what exists, modifying it as work progresses to incorporate ideas for change. Juggling with ideas on paper is less expensive than doing so on the site, although I must stress that a flexible approach should be taken to the plans when working on the site.

The devising of a scheme on paper has another major advantage – it enables you to see if things are in proportion and of a suitable scale. Graph paper is convenient for measuring each existing feature, drawing upon the distances from the house or fence for reference points. If I am lucky, a site plan giving the dimensions of the site already exists – even an Ordnance Survey map can assist.

It is helpful to take a series of isometric photographs from the house looking outwards and from the end of the garden looking inwards. Indeed, I typically write on the back of photographs or even inscribe with marking pen on their front some initial ideas for improvement.

I spend time looking out from the windows of the house deliberating how good the view is from the kitchen, or what those in the dining room would see when sitting down. I also contemplate whether the views look interesting from the bedrooms and go to the farthest extremities and look back at the house. Ideas will emerge as I become familiar with the property, e.g. whether walls may be covered with roses or creeper, and if some architectural features, like the front door, side door or a pergola may be improved without excessive costs to provide a more attractive background for the garden. The garden should also have the right vertical emphasis without the height of the house dwarfing its surroundings. I may find something that needs to be disguised such as a neighbouring house or a distant power station. Furthermore, the sunny spots and exposed areas must be identified.

At least four visits are necessary to nail down features to build on and consolidate first impressions. Occasionally, I am faced with a site that possesses no character. The challenge is to impose a pattern or scheme which creates interest.

I invariably write a detailed report to accompany the plan, explaining the reasoning behind my approach. This method has the advantage of clarifying my thoughts and later reminds me of what I judged important. For the client, it produces a line of reasoning with which he may (or may not!) agree. Details of expenditure will follow once this report has been discussed in detail.

Levels

The first consideration is the general lie of the land, determining whether it is sloping or level, and if it slopes down or up from the house. If the garden slopes steeply down away from the house not much will be visible from the downstairs windows and the view of neighbouring buildings will be magnified. Levelling the area adjacent to the house will, to some extent, overcome these defects. If this course is followed it may be necessary to furnish the boundary of this area with high shrubs or a hedge quite close to the house so privacy within the levelled area may be achieved.

In contrast, if the garden slopes steeply up from the house, views from the downstairs windows will be foreshortened – again it may be desirable to have a levelled area surrounding the house. This enhances the look of the buildings (by settling them in their own space) and an area of relaxation will be provided if orientation permits.

Nowadays, earth-moving equipment can be hired quite cheaply and extra soil may be imported or borrowed from another part of the site, e.g. when building a swimming pool or large pond. If levels are to be changed, generally the choice is between walls or grass banks. It is better to emphasise changes in levels boldly by means of terracing, the building of supporting walls, and the placing of good steps.

Many of the case studies exemplify the advantages that accrue from changing soil levels. In certain situations it was critical to the garden's design – as seen at Ewelme and Bix Hill. In the other gardens, such as White House Farm and the Old School House, it was used to add interest to predominantly flat sites, while at the same time disposing of surplus soil. The logistics of the earth-moving operations are too weighty to be undertaken by an amateur. It is sufficient to point out that on two occasions experienced professionals broke into buried power lines – a memorable experience for all concerned when one incident occurred at 4pm on a Friday afternoon, with a dinner party planned for that evening! Moreover, these huge piles of earth can be the source of discontent for both the team and client. Courage is the watchword here.

Before leaving the topic of levels, I must stress that one of my pet hates is a sunken narrow path next to the house, flanked by a grass bank or wall a level below the lawn. Too often builders of new houses create this feature to save on the cost of wider excavation, creating a cramped corridor which, when viewed from inside the house, produces an uninteresting wall at windowsill level. Generally speaking, the area by the house should be excavated to a distance of approximately 10 feet (3m) as a starting point, after which a series of shallow ledges can be added if the bank beyond still appears steep. However, excavation may have to be even more ambitious so that there is no interruption to the vista.

Existing features

Making use of existing natural features, such as trees, banks, walls and outbuildings, will give individuality to the scheme. They should be emphasised, not hidden, unless they are ugly. There are certain basic rules in the search for good composition:

- ❖ A line across a view gives greater breadth (see Selborne).
- ❖ A line away from the view conveys greater length (see Fisherman's Lodge).
- ❖ Lines away from the view and converging convey even greater length (see Blenheim Cottage).
- ❖ A square in a circle or crescent feels awkward.
- ❖ A gap invites one through.
- ❖ A narrow path feels mean.
- ❖ An enclosed space gives a feeling of secrecy (see The Old Rectory).
- ❖ An excessive variety of shapes or features conspire to disturb the senses, whereas repetition has a calming effect.

Soil characteristics

My earlier discussion on soil excavation should have emphasised the requirement to sort the topsoil from the subsoil. Topsoil is precious and contains most of the organisms and nutrients needed. It should be carefully preserved if an excavation scheme is followed. When the topsoil is in poor condition there are various solutions available. A quick answer is to buy loam soil from a local supplier. A slower but worthwhile option is to improve the soil over time by adding organic matter such as compost, manure or leaf mould. Additionally, I would advise that a composting area should be set aside in any but the smallest garden.

The degree of acidity or alkalinity of the soil needs to be identified before planting plans are drawn up. Some plants, for example azaleas or rhododendrons, detest lime, whereas others, such as herbs, thrive in limey conditions. Test kits may be obtained to measure such conditions, but it should be fairly obvious to the observer whether the soil is chalky (alkaline), neutral or acidic simply by looking around the neighbourhood and seeing which plants thrive. Occasionally, one comes across a site where all three conditions exist – e.g. where a stream has washed through the soil and changed certain characteristics. To generalise, it is best to choose plants that adapt to prevailing conditions rather than seek to change the native soil. Thus, it is not worth adding chemical additives to make the soil hospitable to resisting plant species.

Rooms or zones

Those who have glanced at the case studies will note I often divided the gardens into separate zones or 'rooms'. There is nothing new in this – it is a technique used by many well-known designers including Vita Sackville-West. Division creates a more interesting journey through the garden as not everything is on display in the window – there is a promise of more to be seen inside, of more things to be discovered. Gardens at The Old Rectory and The Leaze gained particularly from this division method, where moods and seasonal effects in each space vary greatly from each other. It is a technique which suits small gardens as well as large, however, it should be executed without abandoning the continuity of style and structure of a good garden. For instance, an existing attractive feature should not be spoiled – a broad sweep of lawn down to a lake should be left undisturbed.

The number of rooms will depend on the size of the plot. It is imperative on a small plot to have one long vista arranged, usually centrally, from which rooms will lead off otherwise the garden will feel foreshortened (Selborne is a good example of this). Hedges will also help to create subdivisions. Other dividing components include walls, trellis, fencing, shrub beds and spreading trees.

Hedges, paths and fences

I have found that as a means of dividing up a garden, hedges take pride of place – as much for economic reasons as for any other. For a new garden they should be near the top of the list of planting priority. It is surprising how quickly a hedge develops. It is a myth that the yew or box hedge will take too long to grow to maturity as a first choice for a hedge. Yews over a metre in height can be bought quite cheaply (from wholesale suppliers) and if placed into well-prepared and watered soil will reach 6 feet (182cm) in three or four years, with a desirable maximum height in five to six years. Yews require decent drainage; the plant must also be kept apart from cattle and horses because it is poisonous. Box hedging is a slower and more expensive alternative, but you will be able to create shapes that beat all others!

Beech and hornbeam are useful for boundary hedges and are cheaper than yew. However, in winter months they do not provide the yew's olive green background that frames daffodils, snowdrops and aconites so beautifully when viewed from a distance. To counteract this blank winter appearance, beech

or hornbeam should be restricted to the perimeter rather than being used as the building block in the garden. Privet tends to have greedy roots and laurel looks butchered when cut close, so I would not suggest them as a priority hedging choice. However, laurel can be attractive as a specimen shrub or tree in certain circumstances. Leylandii is a popular choice for people desiring instant growth, but they generally live to regret it. It grows like a rocket – as much as 3 feet (91cm) a season. Yet, exceptional circumstances, such as blocking a noisy motorway, may call for urgent screening which only Leylandii provides. If a flowering hedge is wanted, then escallonia or cotoneaster are good alternatives.

I have often used 'poor man's box hedge' made from a mixture of *Lonicera nitida* and *Prunus myrobalan* for subdividing hedges of 4–6 feet (121–182cm) high. The insertion of occasional prunus ensures that the main part of the hedge, the lonicera, will stay upright in all winds and weathers. The hint and glint of prunus leaf also lends a pleasing variety to the green of the hedging and in spring provides a white flower. This hedge variety submits well to clipping but needs more regular attention than box, beech or yew. If feasible a double hedge adds strength to the design and provides a corridor which children value.

At the front of the house fencing should be in keeping with the neighbours. Close boarded fencing is the least attractive – park railing and diagonal trellis are favourites of mine.

Walls

I am very fond of walls, having built one with my son. The result was instant maturity – 'a pleasing irregularity' as my friends put it, making a polite virtue of our inexperience.

Including a wall can create a dramatic effect in the garden. Walls at The Old Rectory on the east side of the central section provide a pleasing 'shoulder' which appears to lengthen the view from the house and gives visual support to the garden and house. The wall in the small Glebe Farm Cottage garden bestows an air of antiquity and serves as a means of discreet division of a tiny area. The Moreton Field wall gives immediate privacy to the new terraced area by the front door of the house. The trellis and wall at The Leaze followed a style traditional to that village, making the changed lines look mature from the start.

If a garden has a wall already, cherish it. If bricks are ugly, change them. It is not necessary to knock them down – simply attach thin wafers cut from old bricks onto the surface of ugly bricks. After re-grouting the wall will seem as though it has been there forever. If this operation is performed, the capping will also need to be given attention. I take great care in selecting bricks for a wall which links onto other buildings on a site. Similarly, existing walls made from breeze block or concrete blocks are relatively simple to clothe using wafers of old bricks.

To build a wall from scratch is expensive. Old bricks cost from £400 to £500 per thousand, and bricklayers charge in excess of £100 a day to lay them (2005 prices). However, the effect is incomparable. Capping the wall with rounded bricks (it quickly gets weathered and somehow looks good from the start) and incorporating stone or flint panels into the structure will improve its appearance. Lastly, raking out the joints as deeply as possible will enhance the beauty of the wall and assist climbers attached to it.

Gates, entrances and exits

The first sight of the garden, whether entering from the street or going out from the house, is a matter of keen interest to me – the photographs prove the point without need for elaboration!

The type of gate to be adopted for entering a 'room' (if one is wanted) or the garden is a matter of some importance. A 'see-through' gate of iron may do well here – perhaps bought from a salvage source. I think most designers have their favourite motif. I have used the same blacksmith for 12 years and he has become familiar with my preferred styles for metal gates. A degree of uniformity of pattern within a garden is desirable in this respect.

Terraces

Without exception I have incorporated a terrace into the design of all the gardens in this book – in several instances the terrace has been the principal term of reference. My preferred medium is riven York stone because its texture is so attractive. Occasionally, bricks, artificial stone or gravel have been used, usually on grounds of economy. Wooden decking has recently become fashionable, especially in television gardening programmes, where it is normally suspended over a sloping area to make it level with adjoining rooms. I feel other uses for the medium look rather contrived.

A terrace used to be a status symbol, a plateau affording visitors the chance to be impressed with the vistas of the estate beyond. Nowadays, a terrace more commonly describes an outdoor room where people can sit in dry conditions and enjoy the heat of the sun and the smell of plants. Achieving harmony with the house and garden is part of the design challenge. Siting plants within paving, either in paving cracks or selected gaps in the slabs, is particularly effective. Mint, thyme, prostrate sedum and lavender all lend themselves to this purpose, but keep to a few specimens otherwise it becomes too busy. Treading mint underfoot and releasing its scent is decidedly pleasing.

The terrace should face south or west – it is pointless to spend money on paving an area which is of the wrong orientation. If the back of the house faces east or north it will probably make sense to locate the terrace away from it, against a neighbour's wall facing south for example as with Parson's Rest. Principally, if there is enough space, as large a terrace as possible should be built.

Edging boards

Providing edging boards is helpful for the definition of spaces early on in the project. Later they help to reduce the task of edging lawn with shears. In the past, most edges of borders were supported in some shape or form, usually by tiles, edging boards or bricks. There is still a strong case for installing such supports nowadays, in particular, treated wooden gravel boards, which last for some 25 years, are cheap, and will keep the plot tidy. The dimensions of gravel boards will depend on the lie of the land, but usually a plank 1 inch (25mm) thick and 4 inches (101mm) wide will suffice; this should be nailed to sunken posts placed on the lawn side of the edging board and not on the border side (if it is reversed the job of edging with shears is far more difficult). For a rounded edge, say around the base of a tree, it will probably be easier to use bricks on the edge. Plastic edging does not usually look as attractive, nor does it last as long.

I previously mentioned using edgings for 'definition of spaces' early in the project. A similar effect may be achieved using wire fixed to posts in places where hedges are to be raised, giving some visual emphasis in the early days to the verticals.

The lawn

The lawn should be the crowning glory of the garden, ideally level and large, and in proportion to the rest of the features in the garden. It should also be weed-free. If it is infested by weeds then a thorough weed-and-feed treatment is needed using an accurate chemical spreading machine. Liquid spreading machines do a more thorough job than one spreading solid granules (or lawn sand). These machines are not expensive to hire and are well worth using for the first year or so (my favourite brand is the Walkover Machine by Allen & Co.).

When laying a new lawn, the question arises of whether turf or seeding should be the method used. If an immediate effect is desired, then turf is the solution and with luck it will be mowable within a matter of weeks. However, for a better result, I would suggest using the seeded method. The lawn will be of a superior quality and the work of preparing the soil for seed is no more demanding than that required for preparing laid turf. Ideally choose a grass that is not quick growing otherwise it needs constant mowing.

The choice of seeds will depend partly on the degree of wear expected. In the past, the adage was the less rye grass included in the mixture the better. However, recently rye grass has achieved a more respectable reputation with the development of improved varieties (for use in golf courses in particular), so be prepared to listen to the experts! Essentially, when selecting grass seed make sure that the mixture includes the correct species and a modern cultivar of that species. Check with an experienced expert retailer.

Drainage may be necessary if the lawn is located in a naturally depressed area. In this case the drain should lead to a soakaway in the corner of the garden. However, it should be remembered that drainage often improves as compaction after laying and/or treatment diminishes, meaning less drastic measures than a drain may be sufficient, such as mixing ash and sharp sand into the topsoil where the area has been especially damp.

In order that the lawn achieves its rightful position as the crowning glory of the garden, automatic irrigation should be considered. From the beginning, the garden should be watered regularly during dry spells to keep its uniformity of colour.

Ponds and water features

A properly constructed pond or fountain can add a great deal of charm. They can also draw interesting birds into the garden. The type of pond needed will depend on the position it is to occupy. If space is restricted, a ceramic pot filled with stones and circulating water might fit the bill. Pumps can be bought from most garden centres. If the surroundings are natural and wide flowing, an informal pond may be preferred, but in a more restricted setting, a formal pond, probably rectangular, would be more appropriate. Its placement should bear some relationship to other features in the garden. A formal pond for example, should be placed on an axial line with any door or window on the garden side of the house. An informal pond should be placed where it would be found in nature – not at the top of a slope, but in a valley!

A pool can be constructed of concrete and lined with PVC or a stronger matt black butyl rubber. Another option is to line the base with puddle clay. If PVC or rubber is used it needs to be concealed at the edges by weeping or branching foliage, bearing in mind that water levels drop considerably in the summer. To obtain this foliage, the provision of a shallow ledge around the perimeter is needed where containers may stand – sufficiently heavy to ensure they stay undisturbed just below the water line. The pool will reflect the sky, nearby structures and trees, etc.; accordingly, I always deliberate how to make the best of the reflections. Ferns, bamboo, irises and Japanese maples do well here.

I have found that children love a shallow concrete elliptical pond in the garden, more a saucer – perhaps 4 feet (121cm) long and 2 feet (60cm) wide – where algae, tadpoles and other water beasts can flourish. These little ponds are best located in a shady and informal setting, almost hidden from direct view. Ponds are not recommended if very young children are likely to be left to wander in the garden. If this is a probable scenario, secure covers become vital.

Swimming pools

Of the 50 or so clients for whom I have had the privilege to work, seven consulted me because a swimming pool was to be included in their garden scheme. It is a big turning point when someone decides a pool should be added to their garden. Many questions are asked

- ❖ Where should we put it?
- ❖ How can it be hidden from the house?
- ❖ How can costs be kept to the minimum?
- ❖ What can be done with the excess earth?

I referred previously to the indirect benefit of soil excavation, i.e. it provides an opportunity to change the levels elsewhere in the garden. Even so, a coherent plan for the spare soil is vital.

Generally, the closer the pool to the house the better – it will be used more and the cost of laying water supplies and electricity will be less. It is best to consult an experienced adviser with no preconceived preferences rather than the owners of the house! If the pool can be built alongside an existing building, like a summerhouse or back of a garage, so much the better; it may provide an opportunity to create changing accommodation without incurring extra expense. Good orientation is important, as is the avoidance of shade from large trees. Account has to be taken of the problems which may arise when the builder moves in, such as ensuring access for his plant. There are plenty of specialists available to advise on pool dimensions, I suggest the ideal dimensions should be 30 x 15 feet (9 x 4.5m); the minimum depth at the deep end should be 7½ feet (2.25m). A kidney shape should be avoided. 'Roman' steps are a feature from which young children and elderly people benefit.

Concealing the pool from the house should not present too many problems. The building of a wall or the planting of a semi-mature hedge round the pool will help; yew is probably the best for the latter. Furthermore, redirecting paths and designing attractive gates will make the pool appear as if it has belonged in the garden for a long time.

The cost of swimming pools can vary greatly. The liner pools are cheaper, where a concreted hole is clothed with a layer of plastic, making the pool look tiled. They are excellent value, have the advantage of speedy installation and give the owner the benefit of being able to choose a new pattern after ten years. Tiled (perhaps mosaic) surfaces are more expensive. Pools with automatic covers and solar panels are the most elaborate. Perhaps it is worth thinking about how often you will use it before committing a small fortune!

Finally, swimming pools should be fun – a little gaudiness or artificiality is acceptable. It is not essential to have York stone surrounding the pool. Terracotta tiles, frost-resistant of course, look much warmer and inviting. The same applies to planting: busy lizzies, petunias and pelargoniums can look right in this area of gardening, whereas they may look brash elsewhere.

Pool house designs

There are several examples of pool houses in the case studies. Pool houses make good focal points. They can be bought from garden centres or pool suppliers, but if possible, it is better to add something with a less standardised appearance. The cost of building one from scratch with brick is not that expensive. A budget of between £7000 and £10,000 (2005 prices) should be more than sufficient, unless some very complex plumbing and electrical demands are made.

The pool house on the previous page doubles as a garden pavilion having identical french doors at the rear. The exposed purlins (under the roof line) add interest to the appearance (my inspiration came from Hidcote Manor in the Cotswolds).

Another variety of shelter is the wooden octagonal summerhouse (see page 13) surprisingly cheap to construct if you are handy with a saw. However, it is less easily adapted for housing the pumps and other swimming pool machinery.

Creating focal points

Creating a focal point has been mentioned a number of times as an objective in garden planning. When looking out from the house, or towards any point in the design, the human eye needs to be drawn down lines to a point in the distance, such as an arch, seat, birdbath, summerhouse, statue, dovecote (see page 90), steps, a group of trees, or perhaps a farm gate (not necessarily giving access to anywhere). These will serve to anchor the design – but don't overdo it!

Another type of focal point is a knot garden. It has a distinct claim for its inclusion in this section, used for example, when looking out of a room such as a kitchen, where all-year-round interest is necessary. There are many examples of this in the book.

Topiary

Clipped shapes, large or small, give a garden gravitas and permanence. There can never be too many of them since they catch the eye boldly in all seasons, particularly in winter.

When we bought The Old Rectory, there were several large overgrown holly trees dotted about the garden. It was quite simple to convert the holly tree into pudding-shaped topiary – we simply cut it down and waited for it to bush out again, which it did within three years!

Anyone leafing through the case studies will observe the impact created by clipping plants and shrubs into ornamental shapes. Nevertheless, it should not be regarded as only the province of the bigger gardens – a cottage garden may benefit equally from such treatment.

Where a parterre is created, topiary is an essential ingredient. A series of drums or cones of yew alongside a drive makes the distance seem greater than it is in reality. In America, topiary, especially in front gardens, is very popular. However, regular clipping can be burdensome, so it pays to invest in a light mechanical trimmer. The annual pruning of ordinary shrubs such as *Spirea arguta*, cistus and junipers can also achieve attractive contours if done in a specific way – 'topiarising' in a general sense.

With patience a topiary shape can be achieved from rosemary, spirea, yew, winter jasmine, choisya and prostrate juniper – the latter can be a striking feature at the top of steps. We also decided to create yew buttresses against the front of the house which have almost reached a desired height.

There is a case for creating large green balls of box as focal points at the extreme corners of herbaceous beds or at the sides or corners of paths. They serve to anchor the feature in which they are placed and look particularly good in winter when there is little else around. A frosty or snowy day makes these features stand out well.

Steps

The use of steps in landscaping has been traced to the 15th century, when grand staircases and balustrades linked gardens to imposing buildings. There is no doubt steps give drama to a landscape. Accordingly, they deserve maximum attention and warrant as much expense as can be afforded.

To impress new identity on a flat and uninteresting garden, a series of tiers or different levels may have to be introduced into the site. Bold use of steps can create focal points, whether formal or informal. Large real stone slabs are favourites – their rusticity being an immediate advantage. Railway sleepers are cheaper and a bolder alternative, but better in an informal setting, like woodland.

From a planting viewpoint, steps can be turned into a work of art. Bushy shrubs should flank the steps, such as euphorbia, santolina, cistus or rosemary. There may be scope for planting low crawlers between the tread and the riser, or in other crevices left by the builder, like creeping mint, thyme, sedum and campanula – preferably keeping to a single specimen for maximum impact.

Cost of upkeep

According to Mrs Jekyll: 'If the garden is larger than he can individually plan and look after then he is no longer its master but its slave – just as surely as the rich man is the slave and not the master of his superfluous wealth'. A garden must not be made so large and elaborate that it becomes a burden to the owner. Rock gardens for example, used to be popular features, but are labour-intensive. To some, a vegetable or kitchen garden takes pride of place – the owners gain more enjoyment from producing their own food than from any other aspect of gardening. Yet, I must emphasise that vegetable gardens demand many hours of hard work.

To strike a more positive note, there are features such as trees, gravel gardens, terraces and shrubs, which are pleasing to look at and undemanding in terms of labour. A tree, such as a winter-flowering cherry (*Prunus subhirtella*), is a joy to behold in all but the smallest garden. Gravel gardens require little maintenance and enjoy all the attractions of big flower borders. The secret is to prepare them well using a plastic water-imbibing diaphragm under the gravel.

To conclude, there are many ways that a garden can be designed to limit the load on the owner with regard to its upkeep.

Planning permission

Many kinds of building and structure can be built in the garden or on the land around the house without the need to apply for planning permission. These include sheds, greenhouses, summerhouses, swimming pools, ponds, tennis courts and many other structures. However, planning permission is required in the following cases:

❖ If you want to erect a building which is more than 3 metres high or more than 4 metres high if it has a ridged roof (measured from the highest ground adjacent to it).
❖ If you live in a Conservation Area, a National Park, or an area designated as an Area of Outstanding Natural Beauty and want to construct a building with a volume of more than 10 cubic metres.
❖ If you wish to erect a wall or fence over 2 metres high.

Planting hedges and trees does not require planning permission.

The above guidance is not comprehensive but covers most topics touched upon in this book. Obviously, neighbours' views should be sought if they are likely to be affected by any changes.

Getting started – logistics

Once the plan has been prepared, the task of transferring it on the ground follows. If major changes to the gradients are involved, the help of a professional is advisable – he will be able to assess the task, including the possibility of electric lines and drainage etc. being disturbed. Otherwise you may be able to implement the plan yourself:

1. Mark the broad outlines on the ground of the reshaping intended.
2. The position of paths, fences, steps and borders can be indicated using 'upside down' marking paint.
3. If the gradients are to be changed, the 'cut and fill' method can be used, or imported soil may be brought in (the latter is more expensive).
4. If a border is to be created from a grassed area it is easier to mark it out then kill unwanted grass using a chemical grass and weed killer (such as Roundup). The area can then be dug over with a layer of manure or compost mixed in while digging.
5. If brick edges are to be used, add them before planting (the same applies to paths).
6. Where hedges are planted, erecting a temporary light fence made from strands of wire fixed to posts has the double advantage of giving vertical interest and temporary support.

Using natural materials and original designs

If the budget allows, try to acquire original artefacts and natural materials rather than standard or artificial ones. Artificial stone substitutes, ready-made sheds, pergolas, gates and arches bought from a catalogue, all conspire to make a garden look much like many others. Using natural materials is not always more costly than substitutes, and certainly a handbuilt pergola or summerhouse looks infinitely more elegant than a machine-made example. The American fashion of putting roof trusses onto a pergola is rather attractive, especially if it creates a focal point in the garden. For a terrace, natural stone or real bricks should preferably be used.

The choice of material for paths will depend on the resources available; bricks look good as edging paths (see photograph) and indeed in a small garden give a stylish structure if used exclusively for pathing. Gravel or pea shingle has that warm colour, more attractive than say crushed stone, but it needs upkeep – on a muddy day, stones may inadvertently end up being carried into the house on the bottom of shoes etc. Gravel can be used initially while saving for other more attractive mediums. Concrete tarmac should be resisted – a driveway need not look like a mini-highway. Dividing the drive into two strips with grass in between will soften its contours dramatically.

How to generate ideas

I am often asked how to generate ideas for improving gardens. The following should be borne in mind:

- ❖ Few plots are perfect – as with other aspects of life, compromise is often the order of the day.
- ❖ You must be an optimist. You may buy a plant or shrub in a jiffy pot, but it takes great optimism to envisage its final effect in the garden.
- ❖ You must persevere; mistakes will be made but can be corrected. Any feature needing alteration must be noted, so when autumn arrives, plants may be divided, moved, or dug up without killing them.

I would advise browsing through gardening publications to provide ideas for a theme, or for solving a particular problem in your garden such as achieving the correct approach to the house. It helps to collect reference books and to create scrapbooks into which good magazine and newspaper articles can be pasted. Visits to other gardens may stimulate ideas. Sissinghurst Castle gardens are, in my view, among the most inspirational to visit – the compartmental garden par excellence. The Scottish estate, Cawdor Castle, is less well known, but full of appeal (see photographs above).

Checklist

❖ Draw up plans on paper starting with the site dimensions. First note existing features then jot down ideas to change the site. Take photos looking from and towards the house.

❖ Make good use of any existing natural features, e.g. variations in levels, banks, trees, walls, outbuildings etc. Consider excavating one area, e.g. to level it, thereby producing sufficient materials to raise levels elsewhere. Maintain the important views. Check the soil make-up.

❖ In a larger garden, dividing the area into sub-plots introduces an element of surprise and provides the opportunity to allocate to each plot a distinctive motif or theme. Hedges provide a green background for the flowering plants and offer protection against the wind.

❖ Edges strengthened with gravel board save on shearing time and add to the symmetry.

❖ The lawn is the crowning glory of any garden – it is worth spending the time to get it right.

❖ Close to the house try to achieve a level area – paved terraces should be located to ensure maximum sun and not necessarily in close proximity to the house.

❖ Ponds can add charm and attract bird life but do take into account the safety of children.

❖ The cost of upkeep should be borne in mind.

❖ Swimming pools, where practicable, provide a catalyst for change by providing surplus earth that can be used elsewhere in the garden. Pool houses should be designed as things of beauty.

❖ Make more use of topiary.

❖ Plant with purpose. Each garden requires individual treatment – do not try to copy a feature seen in another garden unless you are certain it will fit into the existing set-up. The motto should be 'to plant is more important than to build':

➢ Consider whether bold masses are needed.

➢ Plant shrubs and trees that are well developed but not oversized – the latter are usually very expensive and often take quite some time to settle in well. Avoid fast-growing species such as Leylandii.

➢ Group plants or shrubs of the same type rather than introducing too many different varieties.

➢ Planting schemes should be designed to create a proper structure, i.e. to define spaces, to create gateways, to provide a 'softer' edge to existing features, to screen intrusive elements and to provide shelter from prevailing winds.

➢ Planting schemes should create all-year-round colour and interest. Contrasting greens will be of more significance than any other colour contrasts. Lavender, rosemary, thyme and sage are staples and roses have a place in any garden.

❖ Find a wholesale grower/supplier nearby – using retail horticultural outlets is prohibitively expensive for major schemes.

❖ Reduce the visual dominance of the car if at all possible.

❖ 'Design for life': incorporate adequate areas for storage, barbecues, wheelchair access and make gateways and slopes user-friendly, e.g. for motorised machinery etc.

❖ Irrigation extends the flowering season, improves lawn colour and promotes rapid growth in new gardens.

❖ Use natural rather than artificial materials. Gravel will suffice until funds are available to buy the 'real' thing, e.g. York stone – do not resort to concrete copies.

❖ If possible, design your own gates etc. rather than purchase them ready-made.

❖ Last but not least – keep things simple!

III

CHAPTER III

Planting Selection

Come into the garden, Maud,
For the black bat, night, has flown;
Come into the garden, Maud,
I am here at the gate alone;
And the woodbine species are wafted abroad,
And the musk of the rose is blown.

Lord Alfred Tennyson, 'Maud'

Planting is central to garden making, but it is a huge subject. Consequently, I have restricted myself to the very basic role of planting, that of *shaping* the garden. Plants are perceived as decorative items, providing colour and contrasts, yet their role in defining spaces and screening intrusive elements is more significant in the context of garden planning.

There are two distinct phases for planting when creating a garden from scratch. During Phase 1, hedges, trees and plants which give shape, variety and foundation to the garden, are planted; Phase 2 sees the addition of rarer, more personal choices, which make borders distinctive. Phase I plants are most likely to be found at a wholesale nursery; these can be assembled for purchase and collection if sufficient notice is given. Plants for Phase 2 may be selected from the 8,000 plants listed in the *RHS Encyclopedia* or, for the more discriminating, in the *RHS Plant Finder* (both published by the Royal Horticultural Society). They will need tracking down and prior research will need to be done. Plants for Phase 2 have not been included in my selection.

I begin with shrubs. Most were chosen for their floral colour, but their lasting merit is their foliage display, seen especially in deciduous examples which exhibit amazing leaf colour changes through the seasons. Herbaceous plants follow (dividing between 'plants' and 'shrubs' is a subjective exercise), mainly perennials. These are chosen predominantly for their tone, period of flowering and pleasing growth rate. In this list I have included the smaller herbs, some of which, like lavender, are classified as shrubs in nursery lists. Lastly are those roses that have been used regularly in my garden designs. The rose selection is very eclectic and I could easily have trebled the list! Acid-loving plants are not included in my list.

SHRUBS

Aucuba japonica

Undeservedly reviled! An evergreen spotted laurel which brightens a shady corner against a brick wall. The female Longifolia (a plain green form) is a winner. Flowers very discreetly in spring. It is not for the border – it needs to be accompanied by other evergreens.

Berberis (Barberry)

A big family, some deciduous, others evergreen, including *Berberis darwinii* (evergreen low), *B. stenophylla* (7ft/213cm evergreen) and *B. thunbergii* (green) varieties which liven up a shrubbery or back of an herbaceous bed. The flowers are golden yellow, appearing mid-spring, but it is the foliage which is valuable in certain sites.

Buddleia

There are three favourites. *Buddleja alternifolia* – a lovely lilac waterfall! Distinct from other buddleias, with arching and willow-like leaves with long panicles of fragrant lilac flowers in June. Height up to 15 feet (4.5m), but easily controlled. Can be a major feature, if for example, three are planted in a wide circle or long row. Deciduous. Good for 'secret gardens'. Should be pruned after flowering, not left until autumn. B.Lochinch – probably the most telling background shrub for herbaceous borders, with grey leaves and blue spires in midsummer that keep fresh in a manner rarely achieved with other buddleias. Deciduous. Should be cut back hard in autumn. *B. globosa* – a fast-growing tall variety with dark green leaves, useful for making a quick impact. The yellow flowers in late summer are unattractive but easily sheared off. Can grow to 6 feet (182cm) in two years given encouragement, so effective for blocking an unattractive view. Almost evergreen and will reach 15 feet (4.5m) high. Not ornamental.

Buxus sempervirens

The common box with evergreen glossy leaves. Gives a tidy appearance when used as edging. Marvellous as a major evergreen feature when matured to a hedge or large mound. Also useful shaped singly to anchor corners of beds.

Carpentaria

C. californica produces pure white flowers. Best against a wall in full sun. Medium height, deciduous.

Caryopteris clandonensis

Heavenly Blue is a good variety. Deciduous. Autumn performer with blue flowers and nice form. Small and sits well with grey plants like lavender. The golden-leaved Worcester Gold goes well with Ladies Mantle.

Buddleia

Ceanothus

Many types, some are almost evergreen with glossy leaves and massed blue flowers in June (e.g. *Ceanothus thyrsiflorus* Repens, a prostrate variety) while others are tall, such as Italian Skies or Delight. They are not long-lasting, but quick growers which bestow rapid maturity. Best against a wall or fence.

Choisya ternata (Mexican Orange Blossom)

A large evergreen shrub with glossy fragrant leaves, suitable for formal and informal planting. Flowers early spring and again in autumn with white orange-blossom scented flowers – grows to 8 feet (243cm) and looks good when festooned with *Clematis viticella*. Very fragrant. A must for all gardens, looks good by entrances.

Cistus

There are about 20 varieties which sit well at entrances or to the front of shrub borders. *Cistus laurifolius* is dark, evergreen and bushy, with white flowers. It clips to good shapes (5ft/152cm). *C.x dansereaui* is low, almost evergreen; free-flowing white with blotches. Tall. *C. crispus* has grey leaves with bright pink flowers. Good in shade and in dry conditions. Induces a country feel. In cold areas it needs shelter. June flowering. Likes well-drained soil and full sun. Looks good with herbs.

Cornus (Dogwood)

The best are *Cornus alba* Elegantissima, *C. alba* Spaethii and *C. alternifolia* Argentea for design purposes, but there are many from which to choose. They are worth having in a garden since their stems are so pretty in winter. Best effects are obtained when planted in isolated masses, e.g. beside a pool to reflect the stem's colour. However, some look better at the back of a border, such as Elegantissima, which has white-edged grey/green leaves.

Cotinus (Smoke Bush)

Purple-leafed and green/grey-leafed varieties. Both are good, with flowers which look like a mist. Thrives in any soil and eventually grows into a tree. Can be at the back of wide shrub borders, planted as a specimen or under-planted with bulbs. Plays host to a *Clematis viticella*. Flowers July and in the autumn displays beautiful leaf colour.

Cotoneaster

Many subspecies of which *Cotoneaster horizontalis, C. lacteus, C. latifolia* and *C. microphyllus* are the best examples. All are dark evergreen and berried in autumn. *C. lacteus* Watereri has tall arching stems up to 10 feet (3m) and creates a rainbow of red berries between November and March – a must. *C. dammeri* grows at ground level and is good for carpeting in shady places. *C. microphyllus* can be useful as ground cover in a shady shrubbery. The tallest are usually used for adding a 'roof' to a bed.

Cytissus battandieri (Moroccan Broom)

The pineapple tree, unlike normal brooms, has laburnum-type grey leaves and yellow flowers in June; usually grown as a tree against a wall. Grown for its form, scent and colour. It is large and looks good with grey-leafed companions. Reaches 12 feet (3.6m) in a few years.

Daphne

There are many varieties. *Daphne retusa* is good, both for pinkish flowers and scent in May. Some are slow growing, but *D. burkwoodii* is quicker and often flowers for a second time in the autumn. Grows up to 5 feet (152cm) high and is fragrant.

Deutzia

A deciduous, hardy and bushy shrub with a five-petalled flower. *Deutzia rosea* (pale pink) and *D. magnifica* (white) are good specimens for early summer. Quite vigorous growers and frost hardy.

Elaeagnus

The grey/green variety of *Elaeagnus ebbingei* is a useful quiet evergreen for hedging and background. The variegated variety is best avoided. Medium height and flowers discreetly in autumn, but its chief value is a screen, reaching 6 feet (182cm) relatively quickly.

Exochorda macrantha (The Bride)

A spreading pendulous shrub with large enamel-white flowers in May. It needs a green hedge background to be at its best. Nice form as a specimen reaching 5 feet (152cm) in a short amount of time.

Garrya (Silk Tassel Bush)

Garrya elliptica is almost evergreen, with leathery leaves and catkin flowers in late autumn. A male form, James Roof, is the best. Good against a wall but dislikes cold winds in spring. It is tall (8ft/243cm) and best planted by itself.

Hebe

These vary from low clumps (*Hebe pinguifolia* Pagei), medium clumps (*H. rakaiensis* subalpina) to the taller varieties which can reach up to 6 feet (182cm), like *H.* Great Orme or *H. salicifolia*. Mostly evergreen, with bright green leaves and white flowers in midsummer. Marvellous work-saving and ground-covering performers, especially in north-facing situations, although some dislike extreme winters. They are valued for their green clumps in the winter when other plants have died back. They look best in a shrubbery setting.

Hydrangea

These do well in acid or neutral soil in semi-shade. The white Lacecaps can be used to good effect in a mixed border, while others look best in a shrub setting or by themselves, against a shady wall for example.

Hebe

Ilex (Holly)

A wide variety, grown for their foliage and useful as topiary. As a specimen it can carry a fine crop of berries in winter as long as both sexes are present. It is a tall plant which prefers well-drained soil. *Ilex aquifolium* is the best known, with either plain green or variegated foliage.

Juniperus (Juniper)

The finest of these are *Juniperus communis*, *J. prostrata*, *J. communis* Hibernica and *J. virginiana* (e.g. Skyrocket). All produce strong forms of evergreen and a good scent. Some may be used to give vertical emphasis to a structure. They thrive in alkaline and acid soils. When of reasonable size they create a feeling of maturity in the garden. They can be planted as features in their own right or to provide scale and ground cover.

Kolkwitzia amabilis (Beauty Bush)

Produces masses of pink bell flowers early summer; medium in height and spread. Good at the back of borders or as specimens. Deciduous and unfussy about conditions.

Lonicera

This is a large family including the climbing honeysuckle and the hedging *Lonicera nitida* variety referred to in this book as 'poor man's box'. For bush shrubs, the *L. xylosteum* is a useful plant for a semi-wild situation; reaches up to 10 feet (3m) high, is deciduous and bears white flowers in May.

Mahonia

There are various hybrids of which Charity is one of my favourites. Shiny evergreen, grows to 10 feet (3m) and has brilliant yellow flowers in November. They are best grown as single specimens, against a wall for example.

Paeonia

Produces bold foliage and showy flowers which tolerate shade. There are many bushy varieties; they like rich soil and dampish conditions. Flowers early spring. Tree paeonies can grow to 6 feet (182cm) and do best in a sheltered position with neutral or acid soil.

Philadelphus (Mock Orange)

Virginal is the tallest, Belle Etoile has the best habit and Aureus has yellow leaves early in summer. All are good and undemanding. Aureus needs careful placing and massing to look at its best; effective next to purple foliage. Produces white flowers midsummer.

Potentilla

Elizabeth is a good variety with its restrained primrose colouring. They go well with catmint in a walk. They are not as visually pleasing in an herbaceous setting and some varieties seem 'vulgar'. Best grown in groups. Deciduous, of medium height and flowers from June to September.

Prunus lusitanica (Portugal Laurel)

An excellent dark evergreen with interesting white flowers in summer. It can be used as hedging, to achieve a dark mass background, or as a (topiarised) central point in a round bed. Can grow to more than 25 feet (7.6m) quickly, therefore it is good as a barrier.

Ribes (Flowering Currant)

Grows to 6 feet (182cm) and is deciduous. *Ribes sanguineum* has rose-red flowers in April. *R. laurifolium* is evergreen with greenish yellow flowers in early spring. There is also a golden form (*R. sanguineum* Brocklebankii) which looks best in dappled shade. An undemanding shrub which fills a corner and needs no weeding.

Rodgersia

These have thick greenish bronze foliage with white flowers in the summer. Likes boggy conditions. Deciduous and a low grower.

Sambucus (Elder)

Produces bold, golden or purple leaves that create visual interest in a shrubbery. Golden-leaved *Sambucus nigra* Aurea and the dark-purpled variety, Purpurea, are two hardy deciduous types chosen for foliage. Need careful placing to avoid looking too municipal.

Senecio greyi (Sunshine)

Grey leathery foliage, quick growing and useful evergreens which give a cottage feeling to any setting. The yellow flowers are best cut off if they clash with surroundings. Can spread 6 feet (182cm) or more and go well with other grey-leafed plants and herbs. Need thorough pruning to prevent straggle.

Spirea

Favourites are (1) *Spirea arguta* (Bridal Wreath) which has a fountain shape, 6 feet (182cm) high and is a delight to see when flowering white in April, or simply in leaf for all of the summer and autumn; and (2) *S. japonica*, of which Anthony Waterer, with its calming flowers and 4 foot (121cm) height and spread is good. Several smaller versions give a low hummock (e.g. Nana) and can also be effective at the front of a border. Pruning should be done after flowering and not left until autumn.

Syringa (Lilac)

A hardy, undemanding and deciduous plant. Favourites are blue (Firmanent) and white (Madame Lemoine). Look best alone or linked with *Viburnum opulus* which flowers at the same time and has a similar stature.

Viburnum

This is a big family of which the following are key contributors: *Viburnum tinus* is an evergreen bush, 4

Philadelphus

feet (121cm) high with white flowers in April; *V. bodnantense* is tough with a spread of 8 feet (243cm) and produces pinkish flowers October to January; *V. burkwoodii* is almost evergreen and flowers white in April – looks good as a specimen or against a wall; *V. opulus* (Guelder Rose) is a quick-growing, 12 foot (3.6m), deciduous shrub, with beautiful creamy white flowers in May; the Japanese Snowball variety (Sterile) has round whitish green balls 3 inches (76mm) wide and needs space; *V. davidii* is in demand for its low evergreen cover (3ft/91cm). *V. plicatum* Mariesii grows in a tiered fashion with white lacy flowers in spring and needs an isolated position on a bank of a pond for example. It spreads up to 10 feet (3m) wide and 5 feet (152cm) high. Viburnums are so popular because they each have good forms, are soil tolerant and provide all-year-round interest.

Weigela

There are red and white flowered forms. *W. florida* Variegata has pale pink flowers with arching branches. Medium height.

PLANTS

Agapanthus

Agapanthus Headbourne hybrids (blue) are the hardiest for the UK climate. Late summer flowering. Look good in containers, at base of a wall or at a corner of a bed. Like plenty of moisture and sun.

Anemone

The Japanese anemones *Anemome x hybrida* Honorine Joubert has pure white flowers and goes well in a woodland setting (4ft/121cm). Late summer flowering.

Artemesia

Artemesia arborescens is silver and lacy *A*. Powis Castle is grey/pewter leaved. *A. lactiflora* is green rather than grey. These are used for their foliage rather than their flowers and need staking and trimming to keep as compact shapes.

Astrantia (Pincushion Flower)

Excellent for fresh or dried flower arrangements (I prefer Sunningdale, the greenish white flowering variety). The leaves have a novelty form. Needs sun and well-drained soil where it will flower from mid to late summer.

Campanula

Campanula latiflora Prichard's Variety is the best. Produces large heads of lavender-blue flowers in midsummer. Grows up to 4 feet (121cm) high; a must for any garden. Another variety is *C. persicifolia* (Bell Flower) which has spikes of white (Fleur de Neige) and blue flowers (Telham Beauty) that nod rather attractively in midsummer.

Centaurea

The common blue perennial (Dealbata) variety performs well but can be invasive. It is best used at the front of shrub beds rather than in herbaceous borders.

Clematis

Clematis recta is a tall clump-forming herbaceous plant (3ft/91cm), with dark upright foliage and scented white cream flowers; good in any garden. Peveril is a fine example. The climbers are listed separately.

Crambe cordifolia

A tall, statuesque plant, with huge fleshy leaves and big stems bearing tiny creamy white flowers. Good by itself or in the back of a border. Needs a dark background. Once it has flowered in midsummer it looks rather bare.

Astrantia

Delphinium

Familiar to all and too many varieties to mention. They flower in a wide range of colours in early summer and can be untidy later, so need to be placed in the background. Most need staking and perform best in rich soil.

Echinops sphaerocephalus (Globe Thistle)

Grey-green with blue flowers and grows to 6 feet (182cm) high in midsummer. Can be the centre of a dramatic grouping. Deciduous and undemanding in terms of soil conditions, but requires robust staking.

Echium vulgare (e.g. Blue Bedder)

A self-seeding annual which is useful as ground cover in a new border while others mature – good low habit, blue and pink flowers in midsummer, with lance-shaped dark green leaves.

Epimedium

If a number of plants are massed it makes a stylish ground cover in partial shade. Heart-shaped shiny green leaves tinted bronze in winter. *Epimedium rubrum* is a nice form. *Epimedium perralchicum* is evergreen so its winter tints are of great value.

Eupatorium maculatum Atropurpureum

A tall, striking plant which attracts butterflies. Dark pink, late flowering and will grow in most conditions, but prefers moist earth.

Euphorbia (Spurge)

Good varieties are: *Euphorbia characias* Wulfenii. The biggest (5ft/152cm) is Sibthorpii with huge mopheads of lime-green bracts in spring, useful in non-sunny spots as focal points. Dramatic form, almost evergreen. *E. griffithii* has striking amber-coloured heads with crimson stalks and colourful reddish leaves in autumn. Should be grown in big clumps. Fireglow is a good variety. Dies right back to ground in winter. *E. amygdaloides robbiae* acts as an evergreen ground cover and bears low, polished green leaves. Useful in shrubbery or shaded areas as a spreader. Produces lime-green flowers early summer. A must. The sap can cause an allergic reaction in some people so care should be taken when handling.

Filipendula

Filipendula rubra is a vigorous upright perennial useful for damp conditions – soft pink flowers with large jagged leaves which open from midsummer. Grows up to 3 feet (91cm) high.

Geranium (Cranesbill)

There are many varieties of which some of the best are Himalayense, Johnson's Blue, Kashmir White, Kashmir Pink, Endressi Pink, Psilostemon Pink (larger than others) and Macrorrhizum (for evergreen ground cover). Larger clumps look more attractive – a whole bed of one specimen can look fantastic if

space permits. It is possible to find varieties which flower in every month from April to October. They will grow in all but waterlogged soil; however, they do prefer sunny sites.

Gypsophila paniculata (Baby's Breath)

Frothy white plant to be used in the front of a border. Unfussy about conditions but needs sun. Flowers in summer and lasts until autumn. It has a bushy, delicate form.

Helichrysum

Helichrysum petiolatum is best used for temporary ground cover or in containers. Low growing. The leaves are pale green and the branchlets arch attractively. Will need renewal each year unless very sheltered site.

Helleborus (Hellebore)

There are many good varieties: *Helleborus foetidus*, with finely cut green foliage; *H. niger* known as the Christmas rose; *H. orientalis*, the Lenten rose; and *H. corsicus*, which needs more shelter than the others. All are evergreen, perform well when little else is flowering and induce a feeling of 'style'. They perform well in shade, look best in a woodland setting and are self-propagating.

Hemerocallis (Day Lily)

Grassy leaves and usually yellowish trumpet-shaped flowers in spring and summer. Cottage garden feel to them. Do best in moist soil. There are many varieties to choose from including a pure white form, Joan Senior.

Hesperis (Sweet Rocket)

H. *matronalis* is a simple, white perennial (2ft/60cm) which self-seeds like poppies. Good for new borders while others are maturing. Flowers early summer. Has fragrance in the evening.

Hostas

These are valued for their wide leaves of greyish green or yellow and do well in the shade. Low growers (2–3ft/60–91cm). Big clumps of the same variety are needed. Snails adore them so control is essential. Flowers in midsummer; however, it is their foliage which attracts. There are dozens of varieties from which to choose. Suitable for a range of sites from herbaceous or shrub borders to pool sides.

Iris

Upright bulbous perennials with distinctive flowers. There are many types; the 'bearded' variety thrives in alkaline soil. Flowers June to July. Varieties too numerous to list. Suitable for borders, pool sides and woodlands.

Lavandula (Lavender)

Almost evergreen, summer flowering, with aromatic foliage. Lavender is one of the best tempered and least demanding of plants, asking only for well-drained soil and plenty of sunshine. Its habit, foliage, perfume and attraction for bees and butterflies converge well to make it the garden designer's first choice

when selecting plants. It imbues a garden with maturity and style. Lavender works well in individual groups in the front of a border, or set in a long line by a path. Its height ranges from the dwarf (2ft/60cm) to the tall (5ft/152cm). Some form compact bushes, while others spread almost into arabesque shapes. The best medium-sized examples are the blue Hidcote and Munstead; the larger variety is loosely termed Spica or Old English. There is also a French variety, quite different in habit and colour from the former types. Due to the significance of lavender, I offer the following advice from Norfolk Lavender (the founder, Linnaeus Chilvers, was a distant relative): (i) If the soil is acid, use lots of lime when planting and then an annual topdressing. (ii) The roots like to be in light soil; add plenty of sharp sand and peat if drainage is poor. (iii) The plants are unfussy: they do not need feeding, but a little potassium can improve flowering. (iv) Pruning can be hard or light depending on the shape of the bush desired. If the bush has been neglected and become straggly, using large pruning shears, cut the thick woody stems down to 2 or 3 inches (50–76mm); best done in the spring.

Lythrum

Pink clump-forming upright (3ft/91cm) perennial with spikes of pink flowers in midsummer. Good for damp conditions, so will thrive by a pond for example.

Macleaya cordata

A shapely large-leafed grey plant (4ft/121cm) which bears plumes of white flowers in late summer. It needs to be set in big drifts to be effective. Not everyone's ideal, but they bridge the gap between the tame and the wild.

Mentha (Mint)

Aromatic grey-green foliage. Can be invasive – use with caution.

Nicotiana (Tobacco Plant)

Good annuals. Green-yellow and white varieties used for filling spaces in borders. Need sun and well-drained soil. Generally grow to 2–3 feet (60–91cm).

Papaver (Poppy)

The pale pink varieties look best in an herbaceous setting, for example, Mrs Perry, an old pink variety and the newer Kleine Tanzarine. Self-seeds readily and flowers early summer.

Penstemon

A big family, the best are Apple Blossom, Pennington Gem, Hidcote Pink and Garnet (all about 18 inches/45cm tall). Long-flowering plant, from June to September. They prefer full sun and well-drained soil. A must for any herbaceous border; should be grown in big clumps.

Perovskia (Russian Sage)

A handsome blue flower (3ft/91cm) on grey leaves, useful as a late summer flowerer with good foliage; best grown in groups.

Phlomis (Jerusalem Sage)

The best are *Phlomis fruticosa* and *P. italica*. Grown for their beautiful grey leaves and bushy form. They are attractive most of the year; about 4 feet (121cm) high with a similar spread. Need regular shaping; almost evergreen.

Phlox

Herbaceous plant (3ft/91cm) which does well in sun and fertile soil. A big family, *Phlox maculata* and *P. paniculata* varieties are notable. Choose white or pink varieties which perform over a long summer season, avoiding extreme red and pink shades. The dwarfs are also useful on terraces or gravel.

Polygonum amplexicaule (Knotweed, often called Persicaria)

Not to be confused with Russian Vine; 4 feet (121cm) in height with clumps of spiky leaves and red flowers. Best kept separate within a shrub setting.

Rosa (Rose)

A vital ingredient in most schemes. A list of favourites can be found below (pages 124–125) but there are hundreds to choose from so a catalogue should be consulted.

Rosmarinus (Rosemary)

Much more than a cottage plant – a must for all gardens. Three types are *Rosmarinus officinalis* (traditional), *R. officinalis* Miss Jessops (upright, needle-like foliage) and *R. prostratus* (sprawler and least hardy); all produce blue flowers in early summer and sometimes also in the autumn. The *R. officinalis* can be trained into a bushy shape 4–5 feet (121–152cm) tall by regular clipping.

Ruta (Rue)

The best is Jackman's Blue. Grown for their clumpy blue-grey form, not their yellowy flowers, which are best sheared off. They perform best in late autumn. Some people are allergic to the sap, so care should be taken when handling.

Salvia (Sage)

A big group. Grown for their aromatic foliage and brightly coloured flowers. Favourite forms are *Salvia officinalis* Purpurascens and *S. officinalis* Icterina, both blue flowering and well shaped; also *S. nemorosa*, *S. sclarea* and *S. turkestanica*, which are more upright and individual in character. Some of the annuals (e.g. Victoria) are good fillers in a border.

Sedum

Saponaria (Soapwort)

There is a loose, sprawling, pale pink version *Saponaria ocymoides*, which flowers from early summer. The *S.officinalis* with upright (3ft/91cm) green leaves creates the appearance of a cottage garden. Can be invasive.

Santolina (Cotton Lavender)

An important group, the best are *Santolina neapolitana* Edward Bowles and *S. incana*. They have feathery grey/silver leaves, which fit well into herb settings or as an edging plant. The flowers are not the objective and can be sheared off if desired.

Sedum (Stonecrop)

A good performer from start to finish. Fleshy leaves emerge interestingly in the spring and flower late in summer. The best are *Sedum spectabile* Brilliant (light pink) of medium height and larger (darker pink) Autumn Joy. Must be grown in prominent big clumps. They develop through the season from creamy masses to pink pools of colour by late summer. Attractive to bees and butterflies.

Sidalcea

A perennial with purple-pink flowers midsummer, of similar style to the hollyhock. Jimmy Whittet is a good pink version; it has erect stems (3ft/91cm) and bright green leaves.

Sisyrinchium

A semi-evergreen with spiky grey green leaves which freely self-seed. Good for informal settings.

Stachys lanata (Lamb's Tongue)

A very useful low, silvery-grey, ground cover plant, with mauve flowers; beloved by Mrs Jekyll as an edging for herb and rose borders. The non-flowering variety (Silver Carpet) is also excellent.

Thymus (Thyme)

Almost evergreen with aromatic leaves and small light blue or white flowers. It requires sun and well-drained soil. There are many types, from the ground huggers to the taller varieties which make mounds up to 3 feet (91cm) high. They do well on terraces and flower midsummer onwards.

Valeriana officinalis (Valerian)

The pink varieties grow anywhere and induce a feeling of the country. The white varieties light up the border and are robust. They flower throughout summer; excellent in gravel or other informal situations. (They are said to attract cats but I have not noticed this.)

Veronica (Speedwell)

Mat-forming perennials which flower (blue) in early summer. *Veronica prostrata* is useful as ground cover towards the front of shrub borders.

Symphytum

LOW-GROWING PLANTS

Armeria maritima (Thrift)
Good grey-green hummocks for edging; pink flowers in May and June.

Aubrieta
Useful on dry banks and walls; the blue variety is best. Avoid mixing varieties too much.

Campanula portenschlagiana (Bell Flower)
Cascading mass of blue flowers from July to September.

Mentha (Mint)
The lemon mint, creeping mints and the 'carpet' mints, all do well either in terraces or gravel beds.

Nepeta grandiflora (Giant Catmint)
The best of the specimens, Six Hills Giant is a bushy grey repeat flowerer which looks best in a line by a stone or gravel path, or alongside roses. They also sit well with pale yellow interspersed potentilla bushes.

Saponaria officinalis (Soapwort)
Bright pinkish and fast growing for walls etc. A little bright for some situations.

Sedum (Stonecrop)
Many carpeting varieties some evergreen; *Sedum spathulifolium*, with yellow flowers in June is good.

Symphytum (Comfrey/Borage)
A vigorous spreader, has creamy flowers and is semi-evergreen; only suitable for shady or sunny woodland setting. Hidcote Blue variety has blue flowers.

Thymus (Thyme)
The varieties which creep along stone paths and walls are useful for creating a Persian carpet of fragrant purples in summer. They like good drainage.

Veronica (Speedwell)
An excellent example is Crater Lake Blue, another is *Veronica tenerium*, which goes well in front of border; a deciduous and easygoing plant.

Vinca (Periwinkle)
Vinca is stereotyped as 'invasive and coarse'; however, recently nurseries have stocked new white hybrids which are less so and stay confined to their place.

Virginia Creeper

CLINGERS/CLIMBERS

Akebia quinata (Chocolate Vine)
Vigorous and hardy – an alternative to clematis when green tapestry is needed; purple flowers in April.

Clematis
Many varieties: *Clematis armandii* (evergreen with white flowers) and *C. macropetala* (lavender blue) are best for the small garden and do well in a large container. *C. tangutica* (delicate lemon coloured) and *C. montana* (strong white or pink growth) are most used.

Humulus lupulus Aureus (Hop)
A useful yellow-leafed climber, used to brighten up a dull hedge like hawthorn.

Hydrangea petiolaris
A clinging climber with white flowers in June. Good for disguising ugly bricks – quicker growing than one thinks!

Jasmine
Jasminum officinale and *J. nudiflorum*. The former is a white summer climber with a heavenly perfume. The latter is winter flowering with primrose flowers – can look good trained into a mound. There is also an evergreen, Confederate Jasmine (*Trachelospermum jasminoides*), which looks good on a trellis in a town garden for example.

Lonicera (Honeysuckle)
Deciduous Dutch varieties flower well in June. There are many to choose from, like *Lonicera japonica* or *L. periclymenum* Graham Thomas; the evergreen *L. japonica* Halliana has its uses as a good coverer.

Parthenocissus quinquefolia (Virginia Creeper)
Glorius autumn foliage; select the small-leafed variety (*Parthenocissus tricuspidata* Veitchii).

Solanum crispum (Potato Tree)
From June to December the dark foliage is covered with purple clusters of blooms. *Solanum crispum* Glasnevin variety is good. They need sun and shelter to thrive and are semi-evergreen.

Wisteria
Best grown upon a sunny wall; flowers can be white or lilac. Avoid a cold, windy situation which threatens the flowers on frosty days.

PICK OF THE ROSES

American Pillar
Climber Pink with white eyes, an old favourite. Looks good on old apple trees and the like.

Bonica
Soft pink, repeat, bushy plant (3ft/91cm), goes well in a mixed border or alone. Glossy foliage.

Canary Bird
High bush (6ft/182cm) of ferny leaves and yellow dog roses in May. Best as specimen.

Cecile Brunner
Climbing Pink and Shrub White forms both give vigorous performances over a long season (3 x 2ft /91 x 60cm).

Cooper's Burmese
Climber. Single scented white flowers with glossy foliage. Likes southern aspect. Vigorous.

Constance Spry
Pink large shrubber; short season but superb (12 x 10ft/3.6 x 3m) with heavy scent.

County Roses
Low-growing repeaters. Kent (white) and Surrey (pink) are favourites which can be in a group by themselves or mixed into an herbaceous border.

Dortmund
Red vigorous climber with attractive green foliage. Needs a place by itself. Flowers repeatedly; can be pruned to make a shrub.

Emily Gray
Outstanding golden yellow rambler with good foliage and scent (15 x 10ft/4.5 x 3m).

Felicia
A highly scented pink shrub (5ft/152cm) for a mixed border.

Felicity Perpetue
Semi-evergreen blush-pink climber.

Francis E. Lester
Vigorous medium-sized shrub (or climber) with pink and white repeating flower with good perfume. Best as a specimen.

Fritz Nobis

Vigorous light salmon pink shrubber (5 x 4ft/121 x 152cm) with abundance of hips in the autumn.

Kathleen Ferrier

Vigorous shrub (5 x 4ft/121 x 152cm) with deep salmon pink flowers and dark glossy foliage.

Korresia

Bright yellow autumn shrubber, happy to be in cold borders. Medium height.

Moyessii

Vigorous red shrubber (10ft/3m).

New Dawn

Climber with glossy foliage; pale, pearly pink repeater. Hardy and fragrant.

Nevada

Strong white shrubber (8ft/243cm). Strong flowering in June and July; desultory blooms later.

Pink Bells

Pink glossy and low shrubber (3ft/91cm). Goes well with grey shrubs.

Rambling Rector

White rambler; goes anywhere.

***Rosa banksiae* Lutea**

Pale yellow rambler, needs shelter.

Rosa mulliganii

White banana-scented climber, almost evergreen (15 x 6ft/4.5m x 182cm).

Rugosa Roses

These are the healthiest of all roses and make good shrubs and informal hedges. There are double and single varieties which bear large hips in autumn, for example the Blanc Double de Coubert (white) and Fru Dagmar Hastrup (pink).

Silver Jubilee

Soft, salmon pink bush rose (3ft/91cm); flowers freely in summer and autumn.

Smarty

Pale pink procumbent rose (3 x 4ft/91 x 121cm).

IV

CHAPTER IV

Border Design

Find out what plants grow well...
and plant a lot of them.

2nd Lord Aberconway

Planting a new garden is a glorious task. I like to assemble all plants on the site and work from the back to the front of the border. It is easier to have everything to hand rather than leave gaps to be filled in later.

When choosing the contents of a border, I select plants from the Phase 1 list and place them like an artist applying oils to a painting, so that a harmonious structure and atmosphere may be created. A landscape painter often applies Burnt Sienna oil paint, using the colour to delineate structure; this also allows areas that need to be built with colour to be identified. A dark background is selected with patches of light and a gentle transition of colour, avoiding clashing hues. Thus, simplicity is sought – the formula for a garden border! The vertical element in design is a concept more easily envisaged in one's mind than other aspects; clearly the general aim is to graduate from front to back while allowing for some 'bumps' in the overall scheme.

Many of the cases studies illustrated in this book incorporate twin, parallel, herbaceous borders, divided by a path or lawn; ideally these borders should be at least 13 feet (3.9m) wide, but many gardens cannot run to such proportions in which case a compromise has to be reached. Shrubs at the back of these borders are economical furnishings and provide a backdrop for the more showy plants further forward in the bed. Favourite choices for this 'backdrop' are *Buddleja* Lochinch, *Berberis thunbergii*, deutzias, *Cornus alba* Elegantissima, *Choisya ternata* and the larger spiraeas (like *Spiraea arguta*) and kolkwitzia. Lavatera is a quick performer as a backdrop shrub, but it does tend to produce a rather dominant colour, which clashes with the more delicate colours of the herbaceous plants; it should therefore be used as a stop-gap while

others are coming on. There may be an opportunity to use a tall and spreading variety of cotoneaster (*C. lacteus*), which would sit well in the corner of the garden; it is particularly effective in the winter when most other plants have died back or expired. A cottage garden should have a homely image with a lavender walk stretching to the front door and rambling roses spilling over the porch.

Planting schemes should be designed to create all-year-round colour and interest. Contrast of green will be more significant than any other colour contrast.

There is always an element of experiment in plant selection and it pays to keep a month-by-month diary, which allows successes and failures to be recorded. Later, when autumn arrives, failing plants can be uprooted and discarded or repositioned. I deliberately overdo the planting, especially of shrubs – they mature and grow bigger than the majority, so some must be moved or unearthed. The 'overgrown look' is the aim. If plants are purchased from a wholesale supplier it is probably worth the relatively small extra cost.

Pay attention to those species that advance aggressively as they can be a nuisance in a restricted space. Japanese knotweed is the worst example; it looks alluring in a new shrubbery, but its power of colonisation is equal to that of the British in the 18th century. Another is the common Michaelmas daisy – I have seen it push out its more aristocratic neighbour in the twinkling of an autumn.

Realistically, every site demands an individual response, so one should make an original choice.

I have stressed throughout this book that simplicity is a fundamental requirement for a good garden design. It is better to make an impact with two or three shrubs or four or five herbaceous plants of the same variety, than have a scattering of assorted species – even in a small garden. Designing borders with predominating straight lines is essential in a typical narrow site; they create definition and ease maintenance. This does not imply that the circular feature is wrong in garden design, but a ubiquitous amount of scalloped edging is inadvisable because the eye is distracted by excessive irregularity of shaping.

IDEAS FOR SMALL BEDS

FOR ALL YEAR ROUND INTEREST THIS WOULD BE PLANTED UP WITH LOW WHITE ROSES (EG. KENT) UNDERPLANTED WITH TULIPS, WITH BOX HEDGING AND A DELICATE ORNAMENT AROUND 4 FEET HIGH IN THE CENTRE.

THIS BED IS VIRTUALLY ALL GREY HERBS WITH A TALLER CISTUS IN THE MIDDLE. SOME PINK ANTIRRHINUMS OR PERHAPS ALLIUMS CAN BE PUT SPARINGLY INTO THE GAPS TO ADD DISCREET COLOUR. IT WORKS WELL ON THE LAWN, NEAR THE HOUSES AND CAN BE REPEATED.

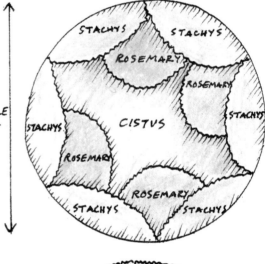

THIS IS A CIRCULAR BOX-HEDGED BED FILLED WITH ACANTHUS (OR ANOTHER FAVOURITE SPECIES WHICH HAS A BOLD LEAF FORMATION AND TALL FLOWERS). A FAVOURITE VICTORIAN STYLE, AT ITS BEST WHEN OTHER BOX-HEDGED BEDS ARE REPEATED IN THE GARDEN.

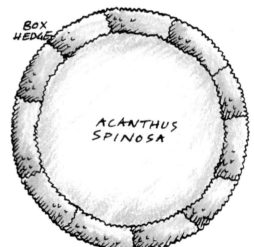

A BORDER AGAINST THE WALL LOOKING WEST OR SOUTH. THESE PLANTS WILL NEED REGULAR SHEARING SO AS TO BE GOOD CLUMPS. THE DOMINANT LEAF COLOUR IS GREY. THE BORDER IS APPROXIMATELY 4.5 m. X 2 m. WIDE. (USED AT MORETON FIELD)

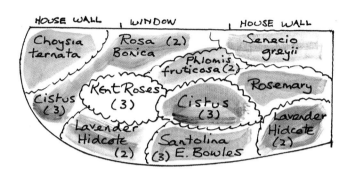

A BORDER AGAINST THE HOUSE IN A SHADY SPOT PERHAPS FACING EAST CAN OFTEN POSE QUESTIONS. HERE IS A COMPOSITION WHICH LOOKS GOOD MOST OF THE YEAR. IT IS BASED ON A BORDER 4 m. LONG AND APPROX. 2.5 m. WIDE. SOME THINNING OUT WILL BE REQUIRED WITH MATURITY. (USED AT SCHOOL HOUSE)

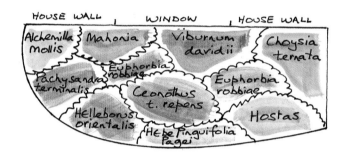

THERE IS OFTEN A NEED FOR A PATH BETWEEN BUILDINGS OR "ROOMS" PERHAPS BORDERED BY A FENCE OR HEDGE. A SIMPLE SCHEME IS SHOWN HERE, SUITABLE FOR A CORRIDOR OF 3.5 m. — 4 m. IN WIDTH. IT PROVIDES COLOUR FROM APRIL — OCTOBER AND PLENTY OF SCENTS WITH MAINTENANCE (USED AT THE RECTORY)

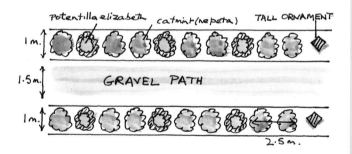

THE ASSOCIATION OF LAVENDER WITH RUGOSA ROSES OF VARYING HEIGHTS IS DISPLAYED AT ITS BEST IN THE GARDENS OF CAWDOR CASTLE. THE USE OF GRAVEL BETWEEN (AND INDEED OUTSIDE) THE ELEMENTS MAKES FOR EASY MAINTENANCE AND GOOD COLOUR CONTRASTS. THE DIMENSIONS CAN BE VARIED TO SUIT THE SCHEME.

I find it helps to have a 'menu' of plants in mind for each sheme:

❖ **Cottage effect:** Anemones; Aquilegia; Catmint; Hollyhocks; Hellebores; Hostas; Irises; Lavender; Pinks; Poppies; Potentilla (Elizabeth); Rosemary; Salvia; Sissyrinchium; Valerian

❖ **Grey/silver foliage:** Artemesia; Caryopteris; Catmint; Cistus; Lavender; Penstemon (big clumps); Rosemary; Roses (procumbent, pink and white); Rue; Salvia; Santolina (Edward Bowles); Stachys

❖ **Screening plants:** Amelanchier; *Buddleja alternifolia; Buddleja globosa*; Ceanothus (various); *Cornus alba* Elegantissima; *Cytissus battandieri*; Roses (various); Portugal laurel; Viburnum (various)

❖ **Background for mixed border:** *Berberis thunbergii*; Atropurpurea; *Buddleja* Lochinch; *Choisya ternata*; *Cotoneaster lacteus*; *Cornus alba* Elegantissima; *Kolkwitzia amabilis*; Lavatera (Barnsley); Roses (various); *Spirea arguta*

❖ **Dwarf spreaders:** Centaurea; Epimedium; *Euphorbia amygdaloides robbiae*; *Geranium macrorrhizum*; Lithospermum; Pachysandra; Pulmonaria; Symphytum (Comfrey); Vinca

❖ **Damp borders:** Acanthus; Astilbe; *Astrantia major*; Delphinium; Filipendula; Galega; Hosta; Liatris; Lythrum; Roses (various); Thalictrum

❖ **Edging plants:** *Alchemilla mollis*; Bergenia; Candytuft; Lavender (various); Salvia (various); Saxifrage (London Pride); *Sedum spectabilis*

❖ **Delicate and ephemeral plants:** Acanthus; Allium (various); Canna; Felicia; Gaura; *Gypsophila paniculata*; Hollyhocks; Macleaya; Miscanthus; Nicotiana; Nasturtium; Solomon's Seal

❖ **Banks of good foliage:** *Euphorbia griffithii*; Lavender; Macleaya; Potentilla; Rugosa roses; *Spirea japonica* (Anthony Waterer)

❖ **Herbaceous bed:** Acanthus; Agapanthus; Achillea (The Pearl); Campanula; *Clematis recta;* Delphinium; Echinops; Geranium; Gypsophila; Hesperis; Iris; Lavender; Phlox; Penstemon; Roses; Rue; Salvia

❖ **Solo specimen plantings:** Ceanothus; Exochorda; Garrya; Roses (various); Viburnums; *Deutzia syringa*

FURTHER READING

From my collection of books about gardens I list below those which I consult most often. Books go out of print relatively quickly and it may be difficult to obtain them new. Second-hand bookshops and out-of-print book search specialists are useful sources of these past treasures. Indeed my favourite book – *Garden Making by Example* by G.C. Taylor (published by Country Life in 1932) – was bought in Dingwall in northeast Scotland.

General interest

The Gardens of Gertrude Jekyll by Richard Bisgrove (Frances Lincoln)
Colour in Your Garden by Penelope Hobhouse (Collins)
Gardens for Small Country Houses by Diana Saville (Viking)
Guide to Creative Gardening (Reader's Digest)
RHS Encyclopedia of Plants and Flowers (Royal Horticultural Society)
Peter Beale's Roses Catalogue (Peter Beales)

Garden design

The Garden Designer by Robin Williams (Frances Lincoln)
The Ultimate Garden Designer by Tim Newbury (Octopus)
Making Gardens [successful gardens listed and described by the National Gardens Scheme] (Cassell)
David Hick's Garden Design by D. Hicks (Routledge & Kegan Paul)
The Essential Garden Design Book by Rosemary Alexander (Timber Press)

Computer design programs

There are various garden design programs available on CD-ROM for PCs which can be of assistance to garden designers e.g. for drawing up the planning grid (such as measuring features from the house, establishing gradients and hardscape features such as brick pathways, fences and walls etc.). They can also be used to particular advantage for translating hand-drawn schemes into final three-dimensional pictures for easier viewing.

INDEX